FAITH AND THE FUTURE

FAITH
AND THE
FUTURE

WALTER KASPER

CROSSROAD • NEW YORK

1982

The Crossroad Publishing Company
575 Lexington Avenue, New York, N.Y. 10022

Faith and the Future is based on the following original works in German:
Zukunft aus dem Glauben, copyright © 1978 Mathias-Grünewald-Verlag, Mainz;
"Die weltverwandelnde Kraft christlicher Liebe," in *Liebe verwandelt die
Welt,* copyright © 1979 Mathias-Grünewald-Verlag, Mainz; "Das theologische
Problem des Bösen," in *Teufel, Dämonen, Besessenheit,"* copyright © 1978
Mathias-Grünewald-Verlag, Mainz.

English translation by Robert Nowell, copyright © 1982,
1983 Search Press Ltd.

Printed in the United States of America

Library of Congress Cataloging in Publication Data

Kasper, Walter.
    Faith and the future.

    Translation of: Zukunft aus dem Glauben.
    Includes bibliographical references.
    1. Theology—Addresses, essays, lectures.
2. Pastoral theology—Catholic Church—Addresses,
essays, lectures.   I. Title.
BR85.K34513 1982   230'.2   82-12720
ISBN 0-8245-0504-2

CONTENTS

PREFACE

It is in the changing situations of history that Christians are continually being called on to give an account of the hope that is in them (1 Pet. 3:15). Over the past ten years there has been a decisive change in the situation in which the message must be proclaimed of the hope that is founded in Jesus Christ. The 1960s and the early 1970s were filled with utopian ideas of evolutionary and revolutionary progress that have meanwhile given way to an increasing fear for the future. As everyone is aware there are grounds in plenty for such fear. But Christians and the churches would have a false understanding of their mission if they wanted to make capital of this fear and exploit it. In this situation too it is their job to point to the one foundation that God has provided in Jesus Christ, and it is their job to bear witness to the future on the basis of their faith.

This can only be done realistically if attention is paid to the powers that are the ultimate reason for fear: despair and the loss of hope. Christians and the churches would once again be ill-advised to pretend that the powers of evil were innocuous or tried to dispute them out of existence through a misunderstood application of demythologization. It is precisely the Christian who is able to look on the powers of evil realistically and without fear and stand firm against them because he or she is aware of the greater power of redemption, which is the only thing that can still guarantee hope in the face of the universal need of salvation.

Hence it was a happy idea on the part of my English publisher to bring together essays of mine on the subject of hope and the future and a larger contribution on the problem of evil. Between them comes a brief meditation on the mystery that is man. Pascal's analysis of human greatness and misery seems to be topical once again today. Theology and the proclamation of the Christian message must always be tested against the touchstone of people as they actually are and their hope.

Walter Kasper

FAITH AND THE FUTURE

One

FAITH AND THE FUTURE

The Challenge of the Future

It is only in our century that the future has become the object of its own field of study. Ossip Flechtheim coined the term "futurology" for this new discipline, starting from the conviction that "a human race delivered over to the dynamic power of technology and science can only succeed in staggering blindly into the future at the cost of deformation or even destruction."

Flechtheim lists five challenges which today constitute our responsibility for the future: (1) the elimination of war and the institutionalization of peace; (2) the removal of hunger and want and the stabilization of population; (3) the overcoming of exploitation and oppression and the democratization of state and society; (4) the end of plundering natural resources and the protection of nature and humankind from itself; (5) the cure of alienation and the creation of a new *homo humanus*.

Taking everything together one reaches the conclusion that what is at stake today is nothing less than humanity's survival in human form. One will only be able to evaluate the situation that has arisen properly if one goes to its root causes. The contemporary crisis is the crisis of the fundamental principle of the modern age. At the start of this age humans discovered their freedom in a totally new manner. They discovered they were not fated to be delivered over to the powers of nature and to the political institutions that had developed, but that they were the responsible masters of their own fates. The development of science and technology provided them with the means to shape their own future. This led to humankind living through far more changes in the past two hundred years than in the previous two thousand. Hence the eighteenth and nineteenth centuries were filled with belief in progress.

Early in our century the belief in progress was severely shaken by the First World War. That was the time Oswald Spengler wrote his widely-read book *The Decline of the West*. The philosophy of existentialism, which arose at the same time, aimed at a fundamental consideration of the insecurity and anxiety that had been aroused. The horrors of the Second World War offered an even more forceful demonstration of the ambiguity and capacity for abuse of technological progress. But concern for sheer survival and the spell cast by reconstruction and economic growth meant that fundamental considerations began retreating into the background after 1945. People felt secure and took too little notice of how fragile the basis for this was until the process of development swamped itself. The continually increasing tempo of change and the ever-growing complexity of our system in fact entail an increasing instability and liability to crisis on the part of our society. If in the recent past we thought we had become the masters of our fate and thought we were able to shape our future ourselves, today we experience our situation as that of the sorcerer's apprentice. Science and technology, intended to serve human freedom, threaten to become too much for us and to turn into a second-order fate. Belief in progress is for the most part being transformed into future shock.

The contemporary situation is therefore to a considerable extent marked by the dethronement of what had been the prevailing ideas of the future. Only two of these ideas need be mentioned here. Almost exactly two hundred years ago, in 1776, the Scottish economist and moral philosopher Adam Smith published *An Inquiry into the Nature and Causes of the Wealth of Nations*, in which he set as a goal an increase in the peoples' standards of living and of welfare. Since then, in those countries in which the industrial revolution has been completely successful, a standard of life has been attained such as could not even be dreamed of by the broad mass of the population in earlier periods of history. It is only today that we have come to recognize "the limits to growth." Even if the details are disputed in the report the Club of Rome issued under that title, people are beginning nevertheless to realize that thinking quantitatively on questions of growth is simply not enough but must be guided by qualitative ideas and principles of human well-being and happiness. That means the end of a purely technocratic model of the future.

This is where a second major idea for shaping the future comes in. Karl Marx replaced the idea of evolution by that of revolution, by which he meant a qualitative transformation of the framework of social conditions. Today this idea of revolution attracts many people even outside the Communist world. But neo-Marxist philosophers have also begun considering the dialectic of such revolutions, which lead to new forms of alienation and create new forms of dependence and new forms of oppression. Above all a revolution cannot answer the question about the meaning of the individual, who is not absorbed by the collective. It has no answer to the question of personal guilt, personal suffering, and death—something everyone must undergo individually and personally. Basically it bisects hope in favor of those in the front lines of revolutionary progress; it ignores those who suffer, those who are oppressed, and those who have failed, both in the past and in the present.

Today, then, both evolutionary and revolutionary belief in progress has been severely shaken, at least for those who are reflective. But the retreat from ideology of the 1950s and 1960s, though warmly extolled, was no less fatal. It was basically only the ideology of the lack and want of ideology. The lack of intellectual perspective created a spiritual vacuum and thus, along with many other causes, prepared the ground for the irruption of radical ideologies and visionary utopias; the violent consequences of these are something we must recognize today with horror. When doubt about the future did not find expression in senseless terror and cynical violence, what often occurred was flight to the idyll of small-scale private happiness, to romantic "back to nature" movements, to the search for immersion in religion and mysticism, to alcohol and drugs, or to a resigned pragmatism based on "muddling through," without any idea of where one was going and relying on the mere art of crisis management.

The crisis is thus composed of a catastrophic absence of meaning, of the collapse of basic supporting values and of comprehensive consensus, and of the lack of far-reaching perspectives and goals for which it is worthwhile being enthusiastic, committing oneself, or making sacrifices. What is emerging in all this is a lack of spiritual orientation and meaning that in the long run can only have a fatal effect. The human person is not merely a being who hopes but a being constituted by hope. No one can live, love, work, and act without hoping and without having a relationship toward the future. It belongs to the essential nature of the human person that he or she is both something given and a project to be fulfilled. For humans the future is the openness that constitutes them; it is the area where their freedom has full play. Hence the future is not what will happen tomorrow and the day after tomorrow: it is a constitutive dimension of the present, the criterion for deciding the why and wherefore of the present, the meaning of humanity today. The present is the future's locus of being; the future is the meaning of the present. When hope in the future is lost, then life becomes meaningless. The question of the future is therefore the locus and model of the question of human salvation. Hope is the essence of salvation.

In the present situation, therefore, none are exposed to a greater challenge than Christians. Today they are asked to give public account of the hope that is in them. They need to authenticate the potential of hope contained in the Christian faith in the face of the questions and anxieties, conflicts and hopes of the world in which we live.

But how should we meet this challenge? Obviously not by following the path of mere restoration, still less by slick and ready solutions and prescriptions. The Second Vatican Council saw the definitive dismissal of the old-style integralism, which claimed to provide the answers to secular questions directly from the faith, and it spoke of the autonomy of secular fields of activity. By doing so the Council accepted the fundamental concept of the modern age and said that secular matters are to be decided in a secular fashion, political matters in a political fashion, economic matters in an economic fashion. None are to be decided magisterially or theologically.

Does this mean that Christian faith consoles people in the face of the great questions of the future by making them concentrate on the next world? Not at all. J.W. Forrester, who developed the prototype world-model that pioneered the Club of Rome's report on *The Limits to Growth,* wrote in an article on "The Church between Growth and Global Equilibrium," "If the moral system does not contain any single institutional component that maintains an open regard for the future, then all social systems are subject to the decay of values with regard to long-term conceptions of value. . . . Apart from religious organizations there are no institutions for long-term goal-projections that are not traditional and point to the future. It is on religions and religious communities that the responsibility rests of maintaining the developing long-term conceptions of value and preventing the destruction of values of this kind."

In other words, the contribution of Christian faith does not occur at the level of instrumental thinking, at the level of the relation between ends and means, but at the level of the determination of the meaning and purpose of what is meant by the future of humankind in humanity. As far as knowledge and the technical means at its disposal are concerned, our age is far in advance of all others. What it lacks are the ideas of the aims for which these means should sensibly be used. It is a question, therefore, of priorities, inspiring ideals, standards of value. Today decisions about these have long been no longer a purely private affair but to the highest degree a public, that is a political, affair. This is where demands are made of Christian faith. What is wanted is not abstract theoretical determinations of meaning but the practical witness of the experience of meaning in life as it is lived. The only thing that counts is the witness of hope that is lived.

The Christian Message of the Future

The theology of the twentieth century began with the rediscovery of the future as the fundamental dimension of Christian faith. This rediscovery is linked to the names of Franz Overbeck, Johannes Weiss and Albert Schweitzer. It was connected with the crisis that in the First World War became evident in optimistic bourgeois Christianity and the liberal theology that represented this form of Christianity. People had, as it were, made themselves comfortable: Christianity and the bourgeois society of the time seemed congruent. Now people suddenly discovered the novel and totally different element, the explosive and subversive element, in the Christian message of the coming of the kingdom of God. They discovered that the category of the new, of promise, of hope, was fundamental for the Old and New Testaments. The biblical history of salvation indeed begins with Abraham leaving his homeland, with Israel's departure from Egypt; it ends with a new heaven and a new earth. The God of the Bible is not simply the unmoved being but the vitally active being who is present, the God who leads us on the way (Martin Buber), a future with the character of being (Ernst Bloch). The Bible calls God "him who is coming."

At that time all this was an exciting rediscovery. Eschatology, the part of theology that deals with the life to come, had been till then a rather wretched and inoffensive treatment of the "four last things" (death, judgment, heaven, hell; including also purgatory and the resurrection of the dead); now it became the all-embracing perspective. If at the turn of the century Ernst Troeltsch was still able to say that the eschatological office was shut, it was now, in the words of Hans Urs von Balthasar, doing overtime. Eschatology became the storm-center of theology. Karl Barth wrote at the time, "Christianity that is not eschatology totally and completely and without remainder has totally and completely and without remainder nothing to do with Christ." Hence Karl Rahner was right in describing Christianity as the religion of the absolute future, and recently Joseph Ratzinger has shown once again that with the rediscovery of the central importance of eschatology the core of what is Christian was re-opened for discussion.

The concept "eschatological" was admittedly overstretched by being made of universal application in this way. In contemporary theology it is used in a variety of ways for everything and anything. Hence the rediscovery of biblical eschatology also opened the door to the ideological abuse of the theological perspective

of the future. After eschatology had destroyed the classical synthesis of Christianity and Hellenistic philosophy, it entered suc-
cessively into alliances with the prevailing intellectual tendencies
of the time.

To begin with, Rudolf Bultmann and his school attempted to
explain Christian hope by means of the categories of existentialism. The future became the future aspect of existence that
is always calling for decision; the real and historical dimension
of time was omitted in this. When in the 1950s economic and
technological growth were recorded on an undreamed-of scale,
we had the wave of enthusiasm for Teilhard de Chardin. Eschatology was understood as a major evolutionary process. The
emergence of the world, of life, of humanity, the advent of Jesus
Christ and the new heaven and the new earth were brought into
one large processive context. The character of judgment and
decision were threatened with being lost in this optimistic and
progressive view. Toward the end of the 1960s the prevailing
optimism then changed dramatically into neo-Marxist inspired
criticism of society. Marxism, in which the primeval power of
Old Testament messianism still lurked in secularized form, was
able to gather to itself many homeless religious energies. From
it arose some new theological projects that were in part extremely
stimulating. Ernst Bloch's principle of hope supplied the categories for the theology of hope and for the political theology
(Jürgen Moltmann, J.B. Metz) closely tied to it. Its aim was to
bring into play once again the public and socially critical character of Christian hope.

Political theology was then developed independently in the
theology of revolution (Richard Shaull, Joseph Comblin) and in
the theology of liberation, or rather in the various different
theologies of liberation. One should not fail to appreciate the
justified concern to be found behind these theologies of liberation in the Latin American situation of poverty and oppression.
It represents a necessary corrective to traditional eschatology,
which was applied in a one-sidedly individualistic manner and
largely ignored the social dimension of Christian hope. Many
tendencies in the theologies of liberation nevertheless jumble
human (political and economic) analyses and prognoses of the

future, as well as human future utopias of Marxist provenance, with the Christian hope in the future. They draw too few distinctions between human well-being and Christian salvation.

This sketch of the history of eschatology in our century—and it is obviously only a very rough sketch—has a reflective air. Theology seems often to have slipped into other people's clothes. This raises the question about what is inherent and autonomous about the Christian hope in the future. It is not as if one could ever present what is specifically Christian in a chemically pure form: all we can do is to express it in human and therefore in historically conditioned categories. There is no theology that transcends the ages. But theology must make critical and creative use of the intellectual possibilities a particular age offers and translate Christian faith into the language of a particular age and into the context of the problems it raises in such a way that what emerges is not some domesticated and suitably adapted Christianity but the challenge of what is Christian. The fundamental problem of this kind of translation of the original message into the language of today consists at the present moment of the determination of the relationship between eschatology and history, between the eschatological future and that which arises from the internal workings of history.

In what follows we shall discuss three points of view that seem to be important for a Christian relationship to the future. In this we shall limit ourselves to the problem of the future deriving from the internal workings of history. We shall therefore not be discussing what, theologically speaking, is no doubt the much more important question of eternal life: we shall be dealing with this life and shall limit ourselves to the consequences of eschatology for the theology of history.

1. The Bible does not just talk about hope for this or that: its concern goes beyond the fulfillment of particular wishes, desires, or expectations. It understands man as a being that not only possesses hope but ultimately is hope. But the Bible is also realistic enough to recognize man's fundamentally finite nature. This is expressed most clearly in death. Death is the only certain thing about our future and hence the critical case for every hope in the future. How then is hope possible? In other words, how

does being human make sense in view of our finite nature? The conviction of the entire classical tradition is that this is only possible when there is an absolute freedom which embraces everything and affects everything, which within and beyond this finiteness keeps a "space" open for humanity, and which embraces both life and death. It is only when God is the reality that determines and embraces everything that our restless striving and searching does not issue in emptiness or in nothing: it is only then that we are not camping like a gypsy on the edge of a world ruled by pure chance, a world indifferent to our suffering.

The future the Bible extolls is therefore not the future that we forecast, plan, and shape, but the future that is given us by God, indeed that is God himself for us. What is involved in the biblical future is therefore not an extrapolation of the present into the future (*futurum,* what is to come) but anticipation, the presence and arrival of God's future, the coming to us of God himself (*adventus*). "My will is to give you a future and hope" means, I, the Lord God, alone can create the future, and not the idols which you have made yourselves and which are only the projections of your own wishes. Paul, therefore, calls God the "God of hope." The future that faith discusses is not the achievement of man but the gift of God. If we had to create our future for ourselves we would be hopelessly overburdened. Because it is given to us we have grounds for thanksgiving (eucharist); we should feast and celebrate. It is not deadly seriousness but humor that is the trademark of Christian hope.

When the Christian says that God is the future of the world and of humanity, then it is not more but less than the non-Christian that he or she knows about the actual future: God is indeed an absolute mystery. Christian hope in the future is therefore neither the prediction of future historical events nor another form of futurology nor an internal utopia. It is not some secret knowledge about the future but rather a certainty about the mystery of the future, a state of finally being hidden away in the love of God from which, according to Paul, nothing can separate us: "neither death, nor life, . . . nor things present, nor things to come . . ." (Rom. 8:38). Thus hope overcomes fear. It sets us free to grasp impartially, dispassionately, and fearlessly what the future actually brings. In this way God's absolute future does not suppress, violate, or replace our historical future but rather sets it free and indeed gives us the courage to cope with it. It is therefore no accident that the historical dynamic understanding of reality that marks the modern age arose on the foundation of Christianity. But this also means that a particular responsibility attaches to Christianity in the situation brought about by this historical understanding of the world. If we are to believe the historian and philosopher of religion Mircea Eliade, Christianity is the only religion that can give meaning and support to a world that has become historical.

2. The only reason God can be the absolute future of the world, humanity, and history is because he is also their absolute origin, because he is the "maker of heaven and earth." Without *alpha* there can be no *omega*. One cannot play *Deus spes,* the God of hope, off against *Deus creator,* God the creator, as Ernst Bloch has tried to do. Rather, Christian hope in the future is indissolubly bound up with belief in creation. Hence Christian hope is not just something purely internal. Admittedly, Christian hope is not hope *of* this world; it is hope *for* this world. It must be tried and tested in the organizations of the world and in responsibility for the world. If it is properly understood and lived, Christian hope is not "pie in the sky," but remains loyal to this earth. This must preserve it from the danger to which it has succumbed so often in the past, the danger of a gnostic flight from, and contempt for, the world.

The danger of contempt for the world is anything but overcome today, and occurs on virtually a world-wide scale with the cynical exploitation and manipulation of nature. The consequence is an increasing devastation of the human environment. Christianity has contributed to this development with its desacralization of the world and its enthronement of man as lord of the world. For a long time theology counted this an honor and merit for the progress of humankind. Today, on the contrary, the philosopher Karl Löwith, the writer Carl Amery, the futurologist Dennis Meadows, and the historian Arnold Toynbee have been the most prominent in making Christianity responsible for the situation that this has brought about. Norbert Lohfink, on the other hand, has recently devoted several articles to tracing the original meaning of the biblical belief of creation. Indeed, he believes he is able to find the ideal of a stable world in the priestly account of creation. Hence he asks how Christians could ever have succumbed to the myth of growth and why they did not take a much harder line with the fashionable prophetic evolutionism. Belief in creation should indeed provide the basis for a new reverence for nature as God's creation and for a kind of fraternal relationship between humanity and nature. Our task of civilization does not mean that nature is surrendered to humanity for ruthless exploitation. Instead it means our task is to cherish and protect nature, and thus to fashion it toward its eschatological fulfillment. Hence, belief in creation is extremely topical today in the context of Christian hope. A totally new chapter of Christian responsibility for the world is being developed here.

The universality of Christian hope in the future finds its most splendid expression in the eighth chapter of Paul's letter to the Romans. Paul speaks there of the whole of creation groaning in travail in its subjection to transitoriness and servitude. In its birthpangs it looks forward impatiently to the manifestation of the children of God, to the kingdom of freedom. Here there is no question of narrowing things down to an individualistic and spiritualistic outlook. The whole of creation, the whole human person, body and soul, the whole of history, and the whole of humanity are included in this hope. The kingdom of God that is to come means at the same time the kingdom of freedom, in which, according to the last book of the New Testament, every tear shall be wiped away "and death shall be no more, neither shall there be mourning nor crying nor pain any more" (Rev. 21:4). These statements would be misunderstood if one wanted to make God's faithfulness to his creation into a substitute for human faithfulness and solidarity and thus produce it as a cheap form of consolation. When human help is possible it must be provided without any hesitation. But situations exist where with the best will in the world no more help is possible, and ultimately, with death, all human help comes to an end. Anyone, therefore, who rules all otherworldly consolation out of order as "pie in the sky" makes this world, too, without comfort or consolation. Christian hope remains faithful to this earth and to man even in those situations where one must look on without being able to do anything.

3. At the center of Christian faith stands Jesus Christ. He is God's ultimate and definitive future. He does not merely proclaim the nearness of the kingdom of God for the poor, the rejected, the oppressed, and the humiliated, but in his miracles he anticipates the new world that has been made whole. In his resurrection the power of death is conclusively broken and the new creation opened. Jesus Christ is therefore the actual realization of the Christian future, its "visible" form, and its lasting standard. Jesus Christ is the foundation and criterion of Christian hope in the future.

In this way the concern of Christianity is not some vague and undefined future: what is at stake is exclusively the future of him who has come (W. Kreck), the actual and definite future of Jesus Christ, his second coming to judge the world and bring it to its fulfillment. The Christian future is the future of him who was crucified: it is thus a crucified future. According to the beatitudes in the gospel it is not promised to those who enjoy power and status in the world but is for the poor, the miserable, the battered, the humiliated, and the persecuted. Christian hope is, according to Paul, hope against all hope. Hence it is never the mere evolution of the present nor simply progress in a straight line. In contrast to the normal human way of seeing things and relating to them which turns on what can be seen and envisaged and achieved, it demands a total turnabout. Christian hope is only possible in faith in the God who brings the dead to life. It is only possible through conversion, transformation, and regeneration. Hence hope and repentance are indissolubly linked together.

Since Christian hope in the future has its foundation in the cross and resurrection of Jesus Christ, it is ultimately the future from the power of forgiveness. It means victory over the vicious circle of evil that continually can only bring forth evil, victory over the vicious circle of guilt and revenge. Through the power of creative love it makes a new beginning possible. Christian hope thus frees people from being victims hopelessly bound to the past and can bridge existing gulfs to open up a new shared future. There is no way forward either in private or in public life without such creative new beginnings in which what is past is forgiven and forgotten and a new common future is ventured. It is shameful that today we Christians have had to be reminded by a great non-Christian, Leszek Kolakowski, that it is not a change of system that is of immediate importance in Christianity but precisely the message that many have discarded as out-of-date, the message of redemption, of forgiveness.

Christian hope as we have presented it here is obviously not something that can be proved or demonstrated. Hope that was proved would indeed not be hope any more. Hope in the future, we said, is the area where freedom has full play. Hence hope can never be merely the calculable extension of objective trends. It is only in freedom that one can decide about hope. It is something one has only to the extent that one involves oneself and puts oneself at risk. Hope is an option of freedom: it is always based on an act of faith. What carries conviction in hope founded on Christian faith is to be found in the fact that Christian hope can include not only the good and noble sides of human beings that encourage optimism, but also their difficult, dark, negative, and evil sides—suffering, guilt, and death. Christian hope embraces the grandeur and misery of humanity (Pascal). It need not deny human grandeur and make being human petty and insignificant, nor does it need to dispute human misery. It can do justice to the whole person and give support in life and in death. In this way hope based on faith is the ultimate truth about the world and humanity.

The Presence of the Future

It is not just today that people ask what has happened to the kingdom of God that Jesus Christ clearly proclaimed as at hand, or ask where God is. The phenomenon of disappointment was included right from the start along with the Christian message of the future. Already one of the later New Testament writings records scoffers who asked, "Where is the promise of his coming?

For ever since the fathers fell asleep, all things have continued as they were from the beginnings of creation" (2 Pet. 3:4). The question is more relevant and topical than ever today, since normally we experience God's hiddenness more than his active presence.

Let us begin by listening to the New Testament, where we encounter not dry and abstract doctrinal propositions but the testimony of experiences. The experience of the presence of the promised future clearly belongs to these experiences in faith right from the start. Jesus did not put his disciples off with the consolation of an indefinitely remote future: he extolled them as blessed for what they were already seeing and hearing. In particular he pointed to his miracles, in which God's mastery was already breaking through to heal and help.

The presence of God's future is expressed in a particularly distinctive manner in something Jesus says about intercessory prayer: "Ask, and it will be given you; seek, and you will find; knock, and it will be opened to you. For everyone who asks receives, and he who seeks finds, and to him who knocks it will be opened" (Matt. 7:7–8). These are astonishing statements that can hardly be reconciled with the logic of everyday life. Normally it does not in any way come about that one who asks receives. The request is rather directed toward a favorable hearing being given only at some time in the future. But in this saying the request not only carries with it the certainty of a favorable hearing in the future, rather the request and its fulfillment are simultaneous. The one who asks receives here and now. The request therefore makes present the favorable hearing in the future. The request that opens and surrenders itself entirely to God becomes in its powerlessness a hollow empty space for God's power: it is the locus of the historical mode of the presence of God's dominion. God's power thus becomes active and effective in the present thanks to the mediation of human freedom opening itself to him in prayer. In this sense the Bible can make the fundamental statement, "All things are possible to him who believes" (Mark 9:23). Faith allows God to come into action: it recognizes his dominion and by doing so makes room for it in the world. To this extent faith participates in God's omnipotence.

It is the anticipation of the eschatological future. It is, as it were, the real presence of eschatological salvation. Hence Jesus can say again and again, "Thy faith hath made thee whole" (Matt. 9:22).

The Bible can also say of love what is said of faith. The most striking indication of this is the well-known discourse on the last judgment in which Jesus says that service to the hungry, the thirsty, the homeless, the naked, the sick, and those in prison is a service done to himself. More, in this service of love the eschatological judgment is anticipated here and now. When someone—whether he or she is a Christian or not—ventures on love expressed in practical help, then he or she already has a share in the world to come. Love is the realization of the world to come under the conditions of the world here and now. In Paul it is the embodiment of the new existence in Christ in which we already participate through baptism. John expresses this idea most clearly when he writes, "We know that we have passed out of death into life, because we love the brethren" (1 John 3:14).

From our considerations so far we can draw the following conclusions. The Christian message of the future is neither a prophecy of future events and developments within the world nor a flight into another world, neither the satisfaction of human curiosity nor the projection of unfulfilled wishes and longings. It is not futurology by other means. Jesus' aim is not to teach us about the end in some cosmological or historical sense but to summon us to commit ourselves to the present, with the end in mind, on the strength of hope. Christian hope therefore opens up a horizon on the basis of which one is given fresh strength to proclaim and master the present. In the horizon of Christian hope the present is not drained of its significance but is rather given its significance back again: it becomes the place of conversion and decision, the place of faith and love. The gift of the future thus also provides the foundation for the task of living as new men and women and practicing truth, justice, freedom, love, and peace. Prayer and work, contemplation and action must here form an indissoluble unity.

The extent to which we must take the here-and-now dimension of Christian hope seriously does not mean that we should reduce the Christian hope in the future to a mere here-and-now eschatology. The present indeed remains subject to conflict, and God's dominion, the dominion of his justice, his freedom, and his peace, is in this world disputed. In this situation Christian hope remains loyal to this world and does not abandon it. Hence it is directed toward a future fulfillment truly capable of achievement. It is not an ideology of the well-filled and contented but rather the hope of those who hunger and thirst for righteousness. It takes on itself the expectation and longing of the tormented creature and waits for the revelation of the future kingdom of freedom.

This leads us to what is probably the most difficult problem of Christian statements about the future: what is the connection between statements about the future and statements about the present? We cannot and need not put forward here all the many theories which have been developed over the last fifty years to answer this question. Our starting point will be the essential nature of what we have described as the Christian future: God himself, who communicates himself to the world and to humans, God in the self-communication of his love. In love present and future are interconnected, for love provides what it promises. This provision does not mean that some kind of claim can be made against it, that it is available and disposable. It remains a gift, the future. As what-is-to-come it is not the abandonment of what-is-now but the entering in of the future, the beginning and start of what-is-new. Statements about the present and statements about the future are therefore interconnected in the thesis that the Christian future is the future of God's love. This thesis means that one cannot simply define the biblical God of the future and of hope as God before us. Biblically speaking God is not only the God before us who makes us flee headlong on the way ahead, but also the God with us, the Emmanuel, who helps us to stand firm in the power of hope of the present.

This presence of God's future and his love the Bible calls the Spirit of God, the Holy Spirit. According to the Bible he is, as it were, God's animating breath that from the beginning is active in creation and creates, maintains, orders, guides, and animates everything. He is at work everywhere in nature and in history;

he is particularly at work when nature and history reach beyond themselves, when something new comes into being. Hence a general and universal outpouring of the Spirit is expected for the end of time. The Spirit is therefore the power of the new creation. It is through him that creation, racked with sighs and expectations, is led toward its goal, the kingdom of the freedom of the children of God. The New Testament proclaims the beginning of this kingdom in Jesus Christ. He is quite simply the bearer and creation of the Spirit: he is God's final and definitive future for the world. It is through the Spirit that God's future in Jesus Christ is to be continually made present anew in history. The Spirit continually places at our disposal, in its novelty, the new thing that is come in Jesus Christ. Hence it is not in the manner of the letter that is dead and dry but in the manner of freedom that the Spirit makes present the person and work of Jesus Christ: "Now the Lord is the Spirit, and where the Spirit of the Lord is, there is freedom" (2 Cor. 3:17). The Spirit is therefore God's personal power over history and the future by means of which God wishes to make us capable of and inspire us to hope, faith, and love in the present.

The Spirit of God is at work wherever someone breaks out of the prison of egoism and devotes himself or herself to other people; wherever someone leaves everything behind, forgets and forgives; wherever someone, on the basis of the ultimate depths of trust, ventures on the future or in silent resignation accepts his or her fate and confides himself or herself to an ultimate meaning and mystery. As Christians we have no reason to think of the Spirit immured in the walls of the churches. We should much rather trust that God's Spirit is at work not only in other churches but also in other religions, in civilizations and historical movements, to the extent that these do not barricade themselves against man's future but rather try to help it come to birth. The presence of God's future through God's Spirit can therefore take place everywhere in the world in many different kinds of ways and often anonymously. God indeed wants everyone to be saved, and that means he grants everyone a genuine chance of God's eschatological future.

These many different forms of the presence of God's future

in history are of course often hidden, distorted, and mutilated. They only become clear and unequivocal when they measure themselves against the standard of Jesus Christ, the actual shape and form of God's future. The presence of God's future therefore becomes clear and unequivocal when people acknowledge Jesus Christ and try to live on the basis of this confession of faith. The church as the community of those who believe is therefore the real place and indeed the sacrament of the Spirit, and thereby at the same time the sacrament of God's future. The church's worship in particular is a celebration in advance of the world to come that makes it present. The sacraments are anticipatory signs of hope.

At this point we come to a stop. To describe the church as the sacrament of hope is for many an empty statement or even one that has long since been refuted by experience. To many the church appears a rigid and static institution, a brake on necessary developments. This resignation with regard to the church and its future is widespread today. For the church, which understands itself as a sign set among the nations, it is fatal. Let us ask therefore what a new way of living out Christian hope in practice could look like.

The Practice of Hope

No actual definite program for the future can be derived from a theology of the future. What such a theology provides, however, are standards, perspectives, horizons of meaning for the actual shaping of the future. Christians or groups of Christians can always be of differing opinions about how this is to be realized in practice. More precisely, two aspects emerge from the message of Christian hope that are important for the living out of hope in practice. Both aspects stand in an internal tension to each other that cannot be suppressed.

(1) *The critical aspect.* The kingdom of God means the future of God's love. It is a future *for* the world, but not a future *of* the world. Hence everything that happens in this world has merely a provisional character and stands under an eschatological reservation. This is only apparently an old-fashioned statement:

in reality it is of considerable topical significance. Its meaning is explicitly critical of ideology. It is saying that no agent within the world, neither a political party nor a nation, no race nor class can set itself up as the agent of world history and anticipate the universal judgment. When totalitarian tendencies of this kind appear, there is need of the Christian's prophetic and critical protest. Insight into the provisional nature of historical movements, therefore, preserves one from fanatical enthusiasms and from enslaving oneself to absolutes one has created. It creates a distance and thus gives inward and outward freedom.

The distance that Christian hope imparts also makes one critical of the ideology of total adaptation to our society seen in terms of necessity, a society which unmasks any hunger and thirst for meaning, truth, and righteousness as false consciousness and which sets as a standard an image of humanity without longings that is quite simply drained of all mystery. At the same time Christian hope thereby contradicts the naive utopia of a society free from suffering. This utopia squeezes suffering into anonymity and makes people mute and insensitive in the face of their own and others' suffering. When suffering is no longer allowed there can be no more comfort or consolation: consolation must be defamed as "pie in the sky." The result is what Nietzsche in *Thus Spake Zarathustra* called "the last man." He is the one who knows neither love nor longing. The great questions of human existence he answers merely by blinking. He makes everything petty and is content with petty happiness. He wants to be neither poor nor rich, wants neither to rule nor to obey: both are too burdensome: "Everyone wants the same, everyone is the same. Anyone who feels differently goes voluntarily to the madhouse." When the spur of hope is lacking humans atrophy.

The reactivation of the critical and liberating power of what is Christian brings to light once more the meaning and importance of some half-forgotten truths of the faith. This applies particularly to the idea of the last judgment, the primitive Christian conviction that every human being and the whole of history stand ultimately under judgment. This idea contradicts our dreams of progress and concord, our delusions of innocence, with which we slip away from personal responsibility. The idea of judgment is therefore something very much connected with the idea of humanity: it recalls our personal responsibility. At the same time, it is saying that in this responsibility all are equal, so that there is a limit to things even for the wicked. The idea of the last judgment is therefore ultimately something that speaks of hope—of the hope that in the end the murderer does not triumph over his victim, the hope for perfect justice (Max Horkheimer).

The idea of the provisional nature of history provides the foundation for freedom in history. This Christian freedom finds its symbolically highest expression in life lived according to the evangelical counsels: in voluntary poverty, voluntary celibacy, and voluntary renunciation of human autocracy. These counsels contradict normal standards and ideas of what is feasible. Correctly understood, they have nothing to do with contempt for the world, but are a witness to ever greater freedom and hope. In particular they are not aimed at a devaluation of marriage. According to the Christian view marriage too is an eschatological sign. But marriage is genuinely free only when it is not the only way of life, when it has not been turned into an absolute, when an alternative exists. Marriage and celibacy are therefore mutually related to one another. Correctly understood, marriage does not mean a devaluation of celibacy nor celibacy a devaluation of marriage. They need each other. And at least as topical and relevant today is a new attitude toward possession and power, toward having things and being able to dispose of them, or to put it in positive terms a new estimation of sharing and serving. If therefore it is ever the case that we can talk meaningfully of emancipation and of freedom to criticize society, then it is a case where what is involved is the realization of the evangelical counsels. The same applies if Christian hope is ever to become an actual lived-out witness. The Christian answer to our present situation cannot be a half-hearted liberalization of what is Christian. The "monks' answer" (Walter Dirks) is topical and relevant today when the hour of the religious orders (J.B. Metz) has come. It could make the church once more into a sign of hope.

(2) *The positive aspect.* The world stands not only under an

eschatological reservation but also under an eschatological promise, the promise of ultimate acceptance by God, of the ultimate victory of justice, truth, freedom, and love over hatred, injustice, falsehood, and violence. If according to Paul it is true that love always endures, then it is also true that everything that happens in history as a result of love endures and is permanently built in to the structure of reality. Everything passes away: at the end we cannot take anything with us. Only what we have done for love has lasting endurance. This means that the Scythian monks of old were wrong when they spent their days weaving their reed baskets and their nights unraveling them so as to get to the other side of the period of waiting for the eschatological future without sinning. Christian hope in the resurrection of the body rather means that what remains at the end is not only a moral distillate that history leaves behind like the pressed-out husks of grapes. In every action in which a person commits himself or herself completely to God and his or her neighbor, in which he or she therefore puts love into action, he or she is already establishing eternity in the midst of time.

Under this positive aspect a number of half-forgotten Christian truths come into play once more. This applies above all to the doctrine that strikes many as rather uncivilized of the merits earned by good works. This doctrine is in truth highly significant from the point of view of the theology of history. It means that what we do, as long as it has its origins in love, goes into building the new and lasting world of the future in a way that cannot be calculated in detail. This doctrine means encouragement for involvement of every kind in the world, whether in the family, in work, in cultural life, in politics, or whatever. It makes one able to accept reality, to accept failure, to demonstrate loyalty and patience. It frees one from the inwardly devouring fear of existence in which one's heart is withered out of shape, and emboldens one to feel joy even in the midst of oppression. If anywhere, it is here that it becomes clear that Christian hope does not mean a flight from the world or a contempt for the world but means the courage and strength to accept responsibility for shaping the world. If under its more critical aspect the impression can be given that Christian hope is only something for monks, it now becomes clear that it can also provide the foundation for a spirituality for lay people in the world.

Keeping one's distance from the world and becoming involved in the world are not antithetical. Nor can they be allotted to different groups of people, to monks on the one hand and lay people on the other. In what of course are different ways they form in the case of both lay people and monks the one basic shape of Christian hope and Christian freedom. It is only on the basis of detachment that genuine involvement is possible; it is only when involvement in the world is respected instead of treated as the work of the devil that detachment is the free renunciation of one value for the sake of a greater and higher value. Freedom for the world and for humanity and freedom for God therefore form an indissoluble whole. The unity of contemplation and action is precisely the shape of Christian piety demanded today.

The Dimensions of Christian Hope

Today there is a "revolution of hope" (Erich Fromm), which affects the future of humanity, the future of human society, and the future of the church. What follows cannot be more than a few scanty indications that need fuller exposition in detail.

(1) *The future of humanity.* Christian hope is hope for humanity, and indeed for every individual man or woman. Every renewal must therefore have its starting-point in the individual. The revolution in thinking about the future that is demanded of us could be reduced to a formula: being more instead of simply having more. In his book *To Have or to Be?* Erich Fromm developed a plan for a whole new society on the basis of the distinction between the two attitudes of existence: "having" and "being." Having means possessing, having at one's disposal, calculating, exploiting, reassuring oneself by tying oneself to the past, a passive attitude of consumption. Being means existing for others, giving, sharing, sacrificing, activity, and creativity, becoming free for the risky enterprise of the future. Behind being and having, therefore, stand different ideas about human fulfillment and happiness.

The furthest humans can go in their ability to be is called by the classical tradition "virtue." The German word for virtue, *Tugend,* comes from the verb *taugen,* to be of use, to be good for. A virtuous person is therefore not someone whose vital impulses are weak and who is afraid of living but someone who has extended his or her capabilities to the utmost because by practice he or she has developed basic attitudes and capacities that make a genuinely human existence possible.

When it comes to determining the contents of this kind of humanly fulfilled existence Christian tradition has had recourse to classical philosophy and has spoken of a set of four cardinal virtues: prudence, justice, fortitude, and temperance. Prudence is something other than dexterous tactical ability. Prudence is neither characterless cunning nor a fanatical insistence on principles. Someone who is prudent is able to see reality without illusions, factually and soberly, and can put his or her basic principles into effect in a way that does justice to reality and to the situation. Prudence is the ability to act in a way that corresponds to the actual state of affairs. Justice, on the other hand, is the selflessness concerned to give everyone his or her own and to be concerned for the good of the whole. For this fortitude is needed. This is the courage and the strength to commit oneself for some major cause at the risk of one's own detriment up to losing one's own life. This has nothing to do with a dashing devil-may-care attitude or with recklessness, but is concerned with the power to stand fearlessly against difficulties. This kind of fortitude is only possible for someone who practices temperance, someone who does not simply surrender himself or herself to his or her whims, impulses, and passions but keeps the faculties of his or her mind and body in order. Someone who practices temperance is not someone who is average or mediocre, but someone whose strength is not dissipated but collected in the service of some important and just cause.

Recently, in a pastoral letter on the subject "Basic Values Demand Basic Attitudes," the German bishops referred to these cardinal virtues and presented them as the tried and tested way to human happiness and as the ways to a new style and direction of life. What is demanded today of Christians and of Christian communities is the witness of the nonconformity of alternative ways of life that are inspired by a greater hope.

(2) *The future of human society*. Christian hope does not apply simply to the individual: it is universal. Nevertheless it is not some kind of political utopia or strategy: "The kingdom of God is not a political norm of politics, but it is a moral norm of politics, and politics is subject to moral norms, even if morals as such are not politics and politics as such are not morals" (Joseph Ratzinger). The most important moral norm for political activity is the fact that the human person is the seedbed, bearer, and goal of all social institutions. The demand that follows from this is for the humanization of all social spheres of life. This kind of involvement of what might be termed "the human system" thus presents an alternative both in the face of those who expect everything to be brought about simply by the transformation of structures and of those who want to maintain the existing structures without asking whether they are human. Referring all relationships back to man—and in contrast to Karl Marx back to man the individual and not to man the abstract species—could be a third way.

Involving the human system demands acceptance of human life, of the dignity of human life, or protecting human life, born as well as unborn, demands a society that has room for children, for those who are ill, for the old, and for the dying, a society that not least has room and opportunities for the future for young people, who today are being deceived about their future to a virtually unprecedented extent—one need think only of the problem of unemployment among young people and the diminished opportunities of work they face.

Being human is indivisible. It means sharing, and today this applies on a world-wide scale. A situation in which the difference between the rich and the poor nations is continually increasing is a scandal that contradicts every single principle of Christianity. It is a basic statement of Christian social teaching that the goods of the earth belong to all people together. The joint synod of the West German dioceses said it was worth paying the cost of our catholicity, the cost of our being the people of God, the price of our orthodoxy. This kind of statement does not actually solve the difficult problem of the just division of the goods of the earth. But it can help toward creating the inner prerequisites and motivations that make people ready to look honestly for such solutions and to make the sacrifices necessary to put them into effect when they have been found.

(3) *The future of the church.* The church is a community of hope. It understands itself as the sacrament of hope for the world, as the place, sign, and tool of the Spirit of Jesus Christ who, according to the fourth gospel, tells us what is to come. According to St. Thomas Aquinas the church's sacraments are signs that point to and anticipate the future (*signa prognostica*), anticipatory celebrations of the coming reign of God. But is the church still understood by people as a sign of hope? Is not despair over the future of society matched by despair over the future of the church? We must stand firm against such questions. The stagnation in the renewal of the church that can be noted today may be understandable after a euphoric period of revolution. But for the sake of the church's future it would be fatal if this development were more than a temporary pause for breath to gather strength. Essential questions about the church's future remain unsolved. There are many starting-points, proposals, and programs for the renewal of the church. Many of them start from renewing the church's structures. No one can reasonably dispute that much remains to be done here. The present stagnation is a fear of the future, a lack of confidence in the Spirit that leads us into everything that is to come. This fear of the future exists among both conservatives and progressives. In the case of conservatives it is because they think the Spirit should work only in the forms already known; in the case of progressives because they give up if he is not at work in the form and at the tempo they expect. Both thus run the risk of shutting themselves off from the actual summons of the Spirit. Yet it remains true that structural reforms cannot be either the starting-point or really the ultimate goal of church reform. They are only meaningful if they arise from and lead to spiritual renewal.

Another path toward the future of the church often tried today consists of the formation of living church communities in which people can experience and celebrate living hope. Again no one can dispute that this is an important task for the future in a society like ours that has become so anonymous. But we should be wary of finding an ideological excuse for silent departure from the church by having recourse to the often misunderstood phrase about the little flock. The way of the small group can only lead forward if it does not lead to flight into the small intimate group, but remains at work within the larger church as a whole. Our thesis is that the national church must become the church of the nation where everyone knows he or she has his or her own responsible share in the church's fate and in its witness of hope. This program can only be put into effect by means of a pastoral strategy of concentric circles, with circles of differing intensity and different kinds of commitment forming around the core community and its core groups.

But now we come to the essential issue: the actual shape in which today and in the future the church's spiritual dimension should in human estimation be articulated. We have already said that the unity of contemplation and action is precisely the form of spirituality demanded today. We shall now take this idea up again and try to clarify one aspect of it a bit more. The thesis is that the future of the church will be decided by its combining the greatest possible openness with the highest possible degree of decisiveness. This thesis stands in contradiction to the present situation of the church, which is torn apart between an openness that, lacking substance in itself, dissolves into a general humanism, and an ossified decisiveness that lives alongside the problems of contemporary men and women without communicating and that ultimately drives the church toward the danger of acquiring the outlook of a sect. The reconciliation of these two tendencies is the spiritual task of the church of the future.

Universality is something that is given with the church's catholicity. At the last Council the church defined itself as the sacrament of the world and gave itself the task of freeing Christianity from the straits of imprisonment in European and North American culture and values and of becoming more world-wide, in other words more catholic. The church can nevertheless only be the sacrament of hope for the world if it gives unequivocal

and decisive expression to its hope, if therefore it does not succumb to an outworn universal humanism lacking the salt of the
discernment of what is Christian. The world does not need its
hope reduplicated, and still less its despair. It needs a determined
church. Being a determined church, of course, demands more
than dogmatic correctness. But more does not mean less. On the
contrary, theological wishy-washiness and minimalism would be
the signs of a faint-hearted retreat and not the signs of an advance inspired by hope. The church can only be a credible sign
of hope if it lives out the beatitudes of the Sermon on the Mount
and if, as a church for the poor, it is itself poor. As a poor
church, possessing nothing but Jesus Christ alone, the church
could be open in a new way. In other words, it only gains its
identity to the extent that it lets itself go; but it can only let itself
go as it should to the extent that it depends totally on Jesus
Christ.

The quarrel between conservatives and progressives that is
crippling the church at the moment is therefore senseless. Unequivocalness and openness cannot be divided into two parties
but form the two beams of a single cross on which the hope of
the church and the future of the world hang. It is only on the
basis of the cross that the church can combine unequivocalness
and openness and be the sign of hope for the world.

Two

THE MYSTERY OF MAN

The Present Crisis

Never before in history has humanity known so much about itself. Never before has the extent of information about itself made it so insecure. Earlier humans knew themselves to be the center, crown, and lords of creation.

This traditional view of humanity has been steadily "demythologized" by modern science. The first blow came in the sixteenth and seventeenth centuries with the discoveries of Kepler and Galileo. It was a real shock to learn that the earth, and thus humanity, too, was not the center of the universe. Humans suddenly found themselves alone in a scattered corner of the universe (Pascal). A second blow came in the nineteenth century. From Darwin's time the theory of evolution has more and more come to prevail. Today the almost universal assumption is of human evolution from the animal kingdom, whatever form this may have taken. The boundaries between humans and animals have become fluid. This meant doing away with an essential distinction to which up till then humans had owed their special position. They now had to recognize that from the point of view of biology they were only "a very small corner of the animal kingdom." Finally, at the beginning of our present century, the disintegration of the old picture of humanity was completed by Freud with his analytical psychology. He demonstrated that as individuals we are not even masters of our own house but are determined and guided by unconscious forces of the Id. The question of our freedom and responsibility thus arose in a new form.

The long-drawn-out, hurt, and furious protest against each step in this triple process of stripping humans of their illusions can be understood only too well. Today this protest has for the most part fallen silent. Modern science has won an unequivocal victory. It has collected a magnificent range of data and insights to give a new answer to the old question: "What is man?" But the more answers there are to this question the less do we know with which answer we should identify ourselves. The larger the number of possible answers, the more we seem indistinct to ourselves as if in a hall of a thousand mirrors. The more we know about humanity the more insistent the question becomes whether we know what is worth knowing about it. Or do we today know more than we used to about the meaning of human existence, about the meaning of love, suffering, and death? The answer is painfully clear. Our life is in spiritual chaos and in a state of confusion that is very close to insanity. Man today is like Robert Musil's "Man without Qualities": increasingly consumed by a variety of individual functions and roles that can no longer be reduced to a single denominator, but afraid of the question, who am I?

There is no shortage of old and new doctrines of salvation that seek to fill the vacuum caused by the crumbling of the western and Christian tradition. Most are simple and totalitarian to a dangerous extent. But more dangerous than such ideologies of salvation is what we have already referred to as Nietzsche's concept of "the last man." The only answer given to the major questions about the meaning of existence is to blink. The question of human happiness is answered by the trivial satisfaction of human needs. Anything beyond that is treated as insignificant. By having become one-dimensional our western industrial society has produced the one-dimensional man (Herbert Marcuse). By means of advertising and propaganda it dangles before us the prospect of the commercial and technocratic fulfillment, or at least the possibility of fulfillment, of all human hopes and longings: from the start it eliminates the question of another dimension of reality. Even in the sciences the question of essential human nature and destiny is for the most part ruled out as unscientific. In a world made up of what can be measured, proved, calculated, and reproduced it has no place. Hence a posthistorical period is proclaimed—an epoch of the dominion of abstract numbers, laws, and structures, an epoch without men and women, an inhuman epoch. For if everything becomes a matter of calculation does not the danger exist ultimately of humans too becoming faceless numbers? Would they then not need to devolve themselves into resourceful animals?

The loss of the humane dimension of human existence is the great danger today. It does not consist of certain historical characterizations of human existence having clearly come to an end. There have been similar revolutionary discontinuities often enough in past history: they also meant the opportunity of expressing fresh and different possibilities for man. The danger is rather of the question about human existence simply dying out. But what first makes us human is that we ask questions about ourselves. From every other point of view we are entangled in nature and in society in a multiplicity of ways; from every other point of view we are determined and manipulated in a multiplicity of ways. But we are distinguished from every other form of life by being aware of this misery of ours and by suffering from it. Our greatness is that in misery we can become a question to ourselves. It is precisely in the awareness of this misery that human greatness becomes visible. Being able to question is the freedom with which a person is able to confront the surrounding world and himself and to say "I." In this question asked about himself a person becomes the greatest mystery for man. If he no longer asked this question, or finally knew what was up with him then the game would be over: as man he would have come to an end: "The solution to the puzzle what man is would then at the same time be the final release from being human" (Jürgen Moltmann).

What Is Man?

We shall try to draw on tradition for the first starting-point in our attempt to answer the question "What is man?" Even if in doing so we establish that today the traditional answers appear totally alien to us, nevertheless there is no other way by which we can penetrate to a new question about humanity except by taking up the unsolved questions of tradition and allowing ourselves to be stimulated by them. The best-known answer to our questions says that man is a rational organism. This classical definition is in practice the common heritage of the entire western tradition. Today it has virtually become a commonplace of criticism that this definition is of its nature in danger of splitting the single object into two constituent parts: the body, which humans have in common with other organisms; and the rational soul, which distinguishes humans from them. This kind of bisection ignores the fact that human intellectual and spiritual nature has a bodily constitution, as vice versa it ignores the fact that the body and sexuality are spiritually and intellectually determined and thus given a specifically human stamp. Body and soul cannot be described as two separate things which only subsequently come together to form a unity. More important than this is a second point of view which makes the classic definition of man appear questionable to us today. It comes from a time when people thought they had at their disposal a more or less exact system of order into which humans could be fitted and by which their essential nature could be determined. Man was considered within an order of nature which existed prior to him, which was built into him, and which provided him with his task. His destiny then consisted of living according to this order. This question once again played a decisive role in the debates over the encyclical *Humanae vitae.* The range of problems connected with the traditional pictures of man became clear to a wider public.

In the contemporary study of humanity there exists farreaching agreement that there is no detailed natural order for human ethical behavior. While all other organisms are instinctively adapted to the surroundings specific to them, humans are "open to the world" (Max Scheler, Helmuth Plessner, Arnold Gehlen). They are the "not yet established animal" (Nietzsche) and must first create their world. Humans are thus not natural but cultural beings. History shows that humans are surprisingly varied and able to change: "Robbery, incest, the murder of children and parents, everything has its place among virtuous actions. . . . The only thing that is certain is that according to pure reason nothing is just in itself, everything varies with the times" (Pascal). Because biologically humans are not self-contained and are open to the world, they are historical beings only able to interpret themselves in a historical process, by means of historical encounter with other people and with other cultures. A distinction thus has to be drawn between what nature makes of humanity and what humanity in history makes of itself (Kant). It is in history that humans must perfect their being and nature. They are *homo viator* (Gabriel Marcel): always on the march, the being of an infinite longing and hope. They could be defined as "indefinability come to consciousness of itself" (Karl Rahner).

It is especially in the modern age that the view has more and more prevailed that the question "What is man?" cannot be answered on the basis of a preexisting natural order but that the task of answering it has been imposed on man himself. This has led to a second historically powerful definition. Since the beginning of the modern age humanity has no longer been considered within the framework of a preexisting natural order. Rather, nature has been considered as the world in which humanity lives, the field of its activity and the raw material of its actions. Humans are indeed differentiated from all other organisms because each can say "I." This means each adopts an eccentric stance (Plessner) with regard to all other creatures, including himself. The intention of the modern age is thus to define man's essential nature not as nature but as freedom. In our century this has been most acutely expressed by Jean-Paul Sartre. According to Sartre there is no human nature at all; existence precedes essence; man is nothing other than what he makes himself to be; man is freedom. His destiny is not subordination and obedience to but emancipation and liberation from the entire preexisting reality of nature and history.

The limits of the modern understanding of humanity are at the moment becoming ever clearer. The "Dialectic of Enlightenment" (Max Horkheimer and Theodor Adorno) is becoming more and more evident. Today it is not man's power but primarily his impotence with regard to reality that we experience. If this reality is still regarded simply as an object for technological exploitation, as the raw material for humans to plan and shape, then it strikes back. Our environmental problems in the wake of technological and industrial development are a clear sign of this. It thus comes about that humanity today is in the situation of the sorcerer's apprentice who can no longer get rid of the summoned spirits. Humans feel they have almost helplessly been handed over to the technological means and to the military technology they themselves invented. The system invented by humans for their own benefit has become so perfect they are now trapped in its cogs and can no longer find their way out.

If one thinks through radically to its conclusion man's utopian stance in and above the world and his homelessness in it, then existing reality is the ultimate in perversity, is radically evil, the "system" that must be totally overcome. Existing reality then comes from the devil. This lands us in a new form of gnosis and contempt for reality. It leads to a cynical exploitation of nature and to a new form of inhuman ascesis, to the pressure to go one better once one has reached a goal by at once setting up new achievements and greater successes. This is the western form of a permanent cultural revolution. But lack of respect for what exists can also lead to a brutal and violent totalitarianism that suppresses present freedom for the sake of a utopian future freedom and sacrifices each present generation on the altar of a utopian future. Both possibilities show that the "hominized world," conceived on the basis of man and for his sake, is not simply already a humane world (J.B. Metz) but instead creates new forms of dependence and suffering and, as it were, produces a second-order fate. The wretchedness of a purely emancipatory conception of humanity is that it can no longer meaningfully integrate and master the suffering and fate it has itself produced. In the face of actual reality it is shown to be abstract. Just as much as the classic metaphysical definition of essential human nature, it fails to do justice to the mystery of humanity.

Criticism of the criticism of the modern age developed after Kant and Hegel and intensified following the left-wing Hegelians. Today we encounter it in a variety of thinkers, in Martin Heidegger just as in Theodor Adorno and Jürgen Habermas. Romano Guardini had already spoken of the "end of the modern age" and had described this end as the end of the modern ideal of personality. In fact, within modern industrial society man's personality becomes more and more obscure and opaque: it disappears more and more behind function and role in the great anonymous machinery of our society. Room for individual shaping of one's life becomes even narrower. In the sense of the personalism that prevailed in his day Guardini's opinion was that in this situation the personality must contract around its core in order to start by rescuing the essential. The question is of course whether such a sublime and purely inward understanding of the person does not remain equally abstract in view of reality. Is not the actual realization of our personality tied to certain natural and social presuppositions? If therefore stress on the inviolable essential core of human personal dignity is not to be a form of romantic escapism, it needs an actual and concrete form of humanism. At present a variety of very different efforts seem to be directed toward this kind of actual historical understanding of humanity. This leads us to a third possible form of human self-understanding.

As men and women we need, in order to be able to live in a human manner, some fundamental concrete preconditions like food, clothing, housing, work, education, leisure, and all kinds of elbow-room for action. The minimum of this actual basic humanity can vary from situation to situation according to the state of intellectual and material development a particular society has reached. But this does not alter the fact that fundamentally humans are creatures of needs and that their freedom can never be a purely autonomous and self-sufficient freedom. Alongside the needs and preconditions that arise from the bodily constitution of our freedom a person's deepest need is to be recognized and accepted by others. Indeed, one must go a step further and say that I can only actually realize my freedom when everyone else respects this freedom of mine and allots me an area of freedom. For its actual realization man's personal dignity demands public recognition. The freedom of the individual presupposes an order of freedom marked by solidarity. As the ancients knew, it is only possible in the *polis,* in community life. Anyone who on the contrary lives outside any community is, according to Aristotle, either a god sufficient unto himself or an animal. Humanity's actual concrete freedom is only possible within the order of law as the realm of realized freedom (Hegel). The fundamentally antiauthoritarian attitude of the anarchists we often encounter today is only apparently "progressive." In reality it is an exaggeration of the bourgeois self-consciousness of individual freedom that is to be realized now and everywhere if only one wants to (Max Horkheimer). For humans, in distinction to animals, "law is the highest of goods" (Hesiod).

But can this historical and concrete understanding of man be enough? Does it do full justice to the mystery of man? Certainly it includes a powerful ethical impulse to commit oneself for the greatest possible happiness of the greatest possible number of people and for a just order among people. But this historical and concrete understanding also includes a utopia, whether as in myths and in Christian tradition the hope of eternal peace (*shalom*), or as in Marxism the utopia of a classless society. But we are still subjected to the dominion of injustice and violence, of falsehood and hatred. What human sense or meaning is there therefore for the people who must suffer and die here and now? What meaning is there for those who are prevented, whether by disease or by external compulsion, from making a contribution to a better, juster, and freer humankind of the future? Is this kind of historical and concrete understanding of man not forced to dissolve the irrevocable dignity of every individual man and woman in the value of humankind as a whole? How can it therefore do justice to the individual value and the individual dignity of every individual man and woman? Must not this view also finally break down when faced with suffering, disease, and death? Does not a historical and concrete understanding of man therefore ultimately remain abstract in the face of the mystery of man?

The Greatness and Misery of Man

Our considerations so far have shown us human greatness and misery (Pascal). The greatness is that humans transcend everything that exists. Man infinitely transcends man. The misery nevertheless is that humans experience themselves as pitilessly tied into the existing reality: "Man is only a reed, the most fragile in the world. . . . It is not necessary for the universe to arm itself in order to annihilate him: a breath of wind, a drop of water, are enough to kill him." But even in misery humans become conscious of their greatness: "Man's greatness is sublime because he recognizes himself as miserable. A tree knows nothing of its misery. Therefore only that which knows itself to be miserable is miserable; but that is greatness, to know that one is miserable" (Pascal). That is a remarkable statement and a quite stimulating sentence; for in the face of all claims to untroubled happiness free of suffering, claims and expectations that modern advertising tirelessly prompts us to hold, Pascal states that true human greatness consists of suffering. "Precedence is almost determined by how profoundly people can suffer" (Nietzsche).

Hence man's existential situation is the mean between two extremes. Man is the creature of the boundary (St. Thomas Aquinas) between nature and spirit, time and eternity, God and the world: "Man is a rope stretched between animal and super-man—a rope stretched over an abyss. A dangerous crossing, a dangerous being on the way, a dangerous looking back, a dangerous shuddering and standing still. What is great about man is that going across and going down" (Nietzsche). Because of this existential situation between the extremes man's essential nature is profoundly ambiguous. The expression "it's only human" can be used to describe the lowest and commonest behavior: all possible weaknesses and vices count as human. But we also use the expression "human" to mean what is highest in our world: generosity, sacrifice, understanding, compassion, forgiveness. Humans are thus a riddle and a mystery: "There are many marvels, and nothing more marvellous than man" (Sophocles).

Human freedom has its foundations in this openness and indecisiveness. But humans cannot actually stay in this openness and ambiguity. If they look into the abyss of their own potentialities, they are overcome by "the dizziness of freedom" (Kierkegaard). Fear seizes hold of them, and they try to cling to what is finite, visible, tangible, and calculable. By doing so they choose what is null and are themselves surrendered to nullity (cf. Rom.

8:20). Humanity and individual men and women, such as we actually encounter and are ourselves, have already alienated themselves from their greatness and destiny. As tragedy is aware, this alienation holds sway over us like an unavoidable fate. All attempts to escape from this situation by one's own power fail. Since we are all subject to the conditions of injustice, violence, hatred, and falsehood, we must from time to time make use of violent means to bring about a just state of affairs. Hence in every new order we automatically include the germ of new injustice, the germ of embitterment and violence. So we find ourselves in a genuine vicious circle of guilt and expiation, injustice and revenge. A qualitative leap, a fundamentally new start is necessary that cannot be derived from the conditions of what has gone before.

Here we come face to face with the profoundest mystery and the real paradox of man. Experience of greatness is tied to experience of misery. Hence humans can never attain their greatness by their own resources. The essential lines of their existence cannot be extended to infinity: they cross each other and turn their existence into a contradiction. What then is man? A torso, a fragment? Does the last word rest with ancient and modern tragedy, with ancient and modern skepticism?

Ecce homo!

When human greatness and misery are taken seriously, when neither hope nor despair is set up as an absolute, when therefore one tries to do justice to man as a single totality, then the question of God must be heard. The opinion that our modern world makes religion more and more superfluous is extremely superficial. It is precisely our modern civilization that in all likelihood will, with the suffering it has itself produced, arouse religious hope to an extent undreamed of before. The soul of religion is indeed nothing other than "the longing for the completely other" (Max Horkheimer), a longing displayed in the ultimate depth of the dialectic between greatness and misery. "It is from dissatisfaction with earthly fate that recognition of a transcendent being draws its strongest power. . . . In religion the wishes, longings, and accusations of innumerable generations are deposited" (Max Horkheimer). "Philosophy can only still be defended in the face of despair if it were the attempt so to regard all things as they are represented from the point of view of redemption" (Theodor Adorno). It is only God, who controls the conditions of all reality, who is able to transform this reality without doing violence to it; it is only God, who is Lord over life and death, who can provide the foundation for hope against all hope (cf. Rom. 4:18), even in the failure of death. Hence at its profoundest the mystery of man is bounded by the mystery of God. He is "the poor reference to the mystery of abundance" (Karl Rahner).

The Christian acknowledgement of Jesus Christ means nothing other than that in him the mystery man, his greatness and his misery, has become the grammar and the mode of utterance of the mystery of God in a unique and nevertheless universally valid manner. It is not as if we could derive their fulfillment from our longing and hope: the mystery of man would then be as exaggerated as the depths of the mystery of God would be misunderstood. We can either accept in faith or reject in unbelief the message of Jesus Christ only as a factual answer to the question put to us by the mystery of our human existence. Every form of argument here must take on the character of appeal, of exhortation, and of persuasion. What is convincing about the form and message of Jesus Christ is nevertheless that it stands the test with regard to both the greatness and the misery of man. Indeed, it is only through Jesus Christ that human greatness and misery are revealed to us in their profundity as in their inner meaningfulness. "It is equally important for man to know this and that; and it is equally dangerous for man to know God without knowing his misery as it is for him to know his misery without knowing the redeemer who is able to save him from it. If one knows only one of these that leads either to the darkness of the philosophers, who have known God and not their misery, or to the despair of the atheists, who know their misery without the redeemer." Through Jesus Christ man can nevertheless come to know both God and his misery (Pascal). This Jesus of Nazareth, as someone who was tortured, mocked, cursed, and put to death though innocent, is the symbol of all those who have been "humiliated and insulted" (Dostoyevski).

God however really showed himself as the "God of human beings" (cf. Heb. 11:16) in the "sacred head sore wounded." Thus it is that with Schelling one must apply to the cross the definition St. Anselm of Canterbury wanted to give of God: he is that greater than which cannot be thought. It is the only possible definition of God and man.

The "word of the cross" (1 Cor. 1:18), "a stumbling block to Jews and folly to Gentiles" (1 Cor. 1:23), is what is distinctively Christian. As long as Christianity wants to go on being Christianity, it is only from the cross that it can find its own definition and destiny as well as its meaning for the world. But what makes one think is the extent to which this cross is continually derided not only in the history of humanity but also in the history of Christianity right up to the present—not so much by theoretical discussions as rather by practical action that knows only one thing, making its own power prevail: "Anyone who sees this and considers it is not amazed that things aren't going well with Christianity" (J. Möller). And yet it is in the cross, today as it has always been, that all Christianity's chances and opportunities are to be found. This sign of contradiction that resists all attempts to smooth it over is not our crucifixion and humiliation. In it, in a completely inderivable and unique manner, the mystery of man has found its universally valid and finally definitive expression. In it, for everyone who accepts it as his or her own cross, a new possibility is opened of being human in an inhuman world.

Three

THE FUTURE OF PIETY

Piety as a Fundamental Human Trait

For us the word piety has taken on the patina of being old-fashioned. It is one of the words of our language that somehow or other has become worn out and the meaning of which today we have to make an effort to discover. If we use the German word for pious, *fromm,* we are usually no longer aware that originally this word meant outstanding, capable. Our usual opinion is that the pious are the peaceful and gentle, those who in a quiet room seek religious devotion, spiritual consolation, and inner security, those who are docile, tamed, measured, who conscientiously and almost fearfully observe religious prescriptions and traditions and try to keep as far as possible from the evil world.

This understanding of piety as something internal and private only arose comparatively recently in connection with the movement termed "pietism" that began among German Protestants in the later seventeenth century. It marked the nineteenth century in particular. One of the great theologians of this period, Friedrich Schleiermacher, defined piety as an emotion, more precisely as the emotion of utter dependence. This interiorization of religion produced lasting religious and cultural values. It was an all too necessary countermovement and protest against externalized religious practice, against purely objective worship without personal participation, against a one-sidedly intellectual understanding of belief. But ultimately this kind of piety that lacked contact with the world was bound to end up by losing touch with reality. The criticism to which religion was subjected by people like Feuerbach, Marx, Nietzsche, and Freud had a relatively easy time trying to dispose of it as merely the semblance of piety. If piety loses touch with the world, the world loses touch with God. The mysticism and the enlightenment of the modern age are related like the two sides of a coin. Modern atheism as a mass phenomenon is, as it were, the reverse of a piety that in practice has become one-sidedly internal and private.

Originally piety—*eusebeia*—was a profoundly secular piety. The religions of the ancient world did not yet experience the world and human relationships in the one-dimensional, functional, and almost superficial manner characteristic of our civilization. Nature had not yet been turned into the object of unbridled exploitation: rather people saw in nature an unfathomable mystery, a divine profundity, something sacred. In the religions of the ancient world piety meant respect and indeed awe in the face of reality, of life, and of the systems and structures on which life depended at family, national, and international levels. We should not be too quick to say that this kind of attitude is no longer possible in an age of science and technology. Many modern scientists—Kepler, Newton, Einstein, Heisenberg, and others—took a similar view. They could not understand the regularities they discovered in nature without an organizing spirit whose greatness amazed them. When this attitude of amazement, of respect, and of piety in this sense is lacking, when people treat reality with a lack of respect and indeed downright cynically, then they destroy the world in which they live, then we end up in the kind of impasse we find ourselves in today. A new awareness of what piety originally meant is therefore something we urgently need today.

Originally piety was not simply the individual's private internal attitude: it was a common public affair, a political entity in the true sense of the term. It found its expression in the joint celebration of worship. Worship and civilization formed a unity. In both people experienced something all-embracing and all-transcending, an ultimate solidarity that went beyond all disputes and conflicts of interest. In keeping with this, offending against piety—*asebeia*—counted as a wanton and sacrilegious offense against the fundamental order of the state and was punished as a capital crime. Here modern tolerance of those with different beliefs does indeed mark progress. But the attempt to provide a religiously neutral and indifferent or rather atheist basis for society and the state is only a very late product in the history of human civilization and one that has not yet stood the test of verification. On the contrary, today more and more voices can be heard pointing out that a society without a minimum of commonly accepted fundamental values cannot last for long. Important sociologists such as Peter Berger and Thomas Luckmann tell us that this comprehensive, universally supported, and ultimately religious horizon of meaning cannot become socially effective without institutions symbolically representing this meaning and thus without generally recognized and publicly religious symbols and rites. At all events a fact worth pondering is that Communist states built on a strictly atheist basis have evidently been forced to create substitute religious symbols and rituals.

We are now in a position to define piety in the general human sense discussed so far as respect for what is holy and divine in reality and as the common publicly recognized linking (*re-ligio*) of the divine to this reality. It is a basic human attitude without which being human cannot succeed in a human manner.

But alongside all its importance for men and women piety is also a dangerous business, an ambivalent entity. Religion has not only its nature but also its un-nature (Bernhard Welte). There is nothing so dangerous as religion. It can congeal into legalism and ritualism, it can turn into anxiety and fear, terror and dread, it can lead to flight from the world and from one's responsibilities in the world, it can make people immature and keep them narrow-minded, it can finally produce fanatical messianism and acts of violence against dissenters. The divine can take on the mask of the demonic. Religious studies thus define it as a phenomenon of contrasts, as *mysterium tremendum et fascinosum,* as simultaneously repellent and attractive (Rudolf Otto). History is full of examples of all this having been and being not just possibilities and dangers but to some extent ghastly realities. It was not for nothing that the prophets of the Old Testament and Jesus and Paul were excessively critical of the religions of their time and of those who were deemed pious. The Christians of the first centuries were regarded by their world as godless, as atheists (*atheoi*), because they kept aloof from the public worship of the state. Early Christianity did not flatly reject the general basic human attitude of piety, but it did subject it to a crisis, a critical examination and differentiation, and provided it with a new foundation and justification on the basis of faith.

Piety on the Basis of Christian Faith

It is significant that when the gifts of the Spirit are listed in Isa. 11:2 the gift of piety does not appear in the original Hebrew text. It was only added later by the Greek and Latin translations of the Bible to make seven from the original six gifts of the Spirit. Clearly the Bible could only take over the idea of piety once it had been purified by being subjected to criticism and had taken on a new quality in distinction to general human piety. Biblical piety is not some kind of diffuse religiosity, as has been revived today in a multitude of forms, but something very definite. For the Bible God is not some nameless mystery, some general idea of the divine, but the personal God who has unequivocally revealed his name once and for all. He is jealously concerned not to be confused with other gods: he is the holy one who may be present in the world but is not simply its numinous dimension of depth but rather is infinitely and qualitatively differentiated from it. Christian piety is simply the reflex, the echo of this understanding of God in people's faith. It is the subjective mode of existence of objective faith, not an activity added to faith. It is man in his totality being affected in faith by God's holiness.

The first fundamental definition of Christian piety is therefore the fear of the Lord. According to the Bible it is the beginning of wisdom. Fear in the sense of awe is something different from the panic-fear of anxiety: the latter is indeed overcome by faith. For that ineffable holy mystery which we run up against everywhere in our lives if only we pay a little attention to the fact, but which ultimately remains ambiguous, reveals itself in the Old and New Testaments as a personal entity who has decided in favor of man and committed himself benevolently to man. God's holiness is at the same time his absolute faithfulness, justice, and love. This at once infinitely differentiates God from us and the world because he is without qualification truth, justice, and love which can be trusted in all situations. The response to God's revelation and the basic attitude of biblical piety is therefore the worship of God's holy mystery. For this there is no need of many words and long phrases. But worship is not a matter of meditating through a glass darkly, of simply contemplating one's own navel, however necessary and salutary this may be and however much such contemplation may be a condition for worship. It is not turning in on oneself to search one's own soul but turning outward and returning to God. Worship means acknowledging God as God and Lord, being moved by God's glory and majesty. Moses removing his shoes and hiding his face before the burning bush, or the prophet Isaiah seeing the thrice-holy one in the vision in the temple, are witnesses of this piety of worship. Jesus himself taught us to pray, "Hallowed be thy name" (Matt. 6:9). In the liturgy we say, "For you alone are the Holy One, you alone are the Lord, you alone are the Most High. . . . We praise you for your glory."

From worship and adoration there grows not servile fear but Christian freedom. This is the second essential definition of Christian piety. The person who finds in God the ultimate ground and meaning of existence becomes free from the power and from the claims to absoluteness of prevailing ideas and theories. He or she becomes free with regard to what the Bible calls the world, by which it means reality turning itself into an absolute and becoming shut in upon itself. The courage for a certain nonconformity, for alternative ways of life belongs irrevocably to following Jesus: it is a part of freedom. This has nothing in the least to do with contempt for the world or resentment against life. Nothing could be more contrary to the biblical understanding of God than this. The person who acknowledges God as Lord must recognize God's gifts and signs of his goodness in all the things of this world: he or she can use them and take pleasure in them but will never be enslaved by them. This freedom from the world is confirmed in freedom with regard to suffering and death. If this life is no longer the end but merely the stage before the end, then one is able to endure this dark side of life with resignation and to accept it with the confidence of faith. Nothing can separate us from the love of God, neither death nor life (cf. Rom. 8:35, 38). But Christian freedom is concerned not only with the relationship to the world and to life but is shown also in our relationship to God. Because God is a God of human beings, our relationship with him cannot be a matter of fearful legalistic piety only concerned with what one is commanded or forbidden to do, a miserable kind of piety that makes one neither free nor happy. Anyone who acknowledges God as Father becomes not his servant but his child, indeed his friend. He or she does not follow some alien law, but the inward impulse of love which recognizes what at any time is the right thing to do. It is the epitome of all the commandments and the essence of Christian freedom. Hence the theologians, headed by St. Thomas Aquinas, see the essential nature of Christian piety in the freedom of the children of God.

This freedom is never something people have for themselves alone but always in solidarity with everyone else. The third fundamental definition of Christian piety is therefore justice. The just person is one who conforms to God's holiness, justice, and truth and who practices justice and truth with regard to his or her neighbor. Indeed, in the Old and New Testaments, "just" is another word for "pious." The prophets highlight this connection extremely vividly: "What to me is the multitude of your sacrifices? . . . Bring no more vain offerings; . . . learn to do good; seek justice, correct oppression; defend the fatherless, plead for the widow" (Isa. 1:11, 13, 17). Jesus claims this tradition: "I desire mercy, and not sacrifice" (Matt. 12:7, citing Hos. 6:6). What is characteristic of Jesus' preaching is the way he joins love of God and love of neighbor together into an indissoluble unity (cf. Mark 12:28–34). Christian piety therefore means prayer and work, contemplation and action. It cannot be refined and keep itself from conflict when it is a question of the struggle against poverty and oppression or of the implementation of human dignity, law, and justice for everyone. It cannot remain neutral with regard to all fronts and tendencies. Piety is mystical and political at one and the same time. It is not for nothing that all martyrs in conflict with political power have become witnesses of the faith. Martyrs of this kind—and the word martyr means a witness to the faith—are to be found today in many parts of the world, in Eastern Europe, in Africa, in Latin America, in China, in Korea, and elsewhere, to a greater extent than ever before. The unity of the love of God and the love of neighbor, of struggle and contemplation is precisely the form of Christian piety that is demanded today.

Lastly, there is a final definition of Christian piety to be found in particular in the later writings of the New Testament, in what are termed the pastoral epistles. In these the Greek word for piety—*eusebeia*—is now explicitly used. What is meant by this term can perhaps most simply be translated as the service of God in everyday life. In this latter stage of the New Testament period the early church met for the first time a danger that would continually become acute for its successor and that still threatens us today: the danger of gnosticism, a rigidly dualistic religious understanding of the world which despises all secular standards and structures. This can lead either to a rigorous asceticism— abstention from food, from sexual activity, etc.—or to a radical casting off of all restraints and complete antinomianism. As against this the later writings of the New Testament emphasize that, because God is the creator of the world, he must be honored also in the structures he has created. For this no special ascetical efforts are needed: everything is good if it is used in the right way. In particular all extraordinary phenomena—miracles, private revelations, etc.—are secondary: they must be examined and tested against the faith handed down. Unfortunately very strong dualistic tendencies have once again cropped up in the history of piety. Often piety has been biased toward the monastic ideal. Christian perfection, however, is measured not by belonging to a particular state of life but by the perfection of love. Piety is not some additional sphere alongside the rest of life: rather it means a way of living that honors God in everyday life and in the structures of the world by a life that is morally good. Piety is not searching for the extraordinary but wants to do the ordinary and humdrum with extraordinary faithfulness: "And whatever you do, in word or deed, do everything in the name of the Lord Jesus, giving thanks to God the Father through him" (Col. 3:17). In this way the friends of God of the later middle ages spoke of finding God in all things.

One could of course derive yet more basic attitudes of piety from Christian faith. But the four attitudes mentioned above should cover the essential core. Consideration of them shows Christian piety to be something very simple and straightforward: the worship of God in Christian freedom which exprses itself in the service of one's fellow-men and women and in the structures of the world. All this sounds clear, simple, and straightforward, and yet it is difficult, radical, and ultimately impossible of attainment. For above everything stands the challenge: "You shall be holy; for I the Lord your God am holy" (Lev. 19:2); "You, therefore, must be perfect, as your heavenly Father is perfect" (Matt. 5:48). But how should we miserable, sinful men and women make God's holiness and perfection, his faithfulness, justice, and love present in this world by our lives? If we wanted to try to do this from our own resources, it would be asking too much and could end only in despair or neurosis. God himself must allow us to share in his holiness and justice. Only if he gives us the spirit of piety can we be as pious as Christian faith demands.

Piety as the Gift of the Holy Spirit

Piety is not something one can make: one cannot plan or organize it. Discovering this is a painful experience for many clergy striving to help others to be pious. Nevertheless one must say it is fortunate that it is so. For the delusion of being able to do and achieve everything, that today has all of us more or less in its thrall, is something profoundly inhuman: it represents a horrible and impossible burden. Ultimately no person can achieve his or her own life: we always have the whole only in fragmentary form. For this reason alone the gospel is already a message of liberation because it frees us from the compulsion of achievement and perfection. What it is concerned primarily about is not what we do but what God does to us. Only he can make us whole and save us. But this means that God accepts us with all our imperfections. Piety is therefore first of all a gift and only thereafter a duty, a grace and not an achievement: it is receptive existence. Indebted existence of this kind involves celebration and joy, and this joy means not only an inner transfiguration, which can often have rather a negative effect, but joy at everything beautiful and good in the world, joy over good human encounters, joy above all at God and his glory. As the New Testament itself shows, this kind of joy can be expressed in a very exuberant manner, in songs and gestures and even in ecstatic phenomena—in sharp contrast to our average Sunday services with their starched formality and low emotional temperature.

The Holy Spirit—as we can say for the moment without thereby being able even to come near to exhausting his mystery— is the personal expression of God's turning to humanity in grace, forgiveness, and reconciliation: he is God's exuberant revelation of himself. He is in person the gift of piety. It is he who, according to the medieval hymn, washes what is dirty, refreshes what is dry, heals what is wounded, bends what is stiff, warms what is cold, guides what has gone astray. Probably many people will have difficulties at this point and ask how one should actually conceive this gift of the Spirit. They will say skeptically that it is all nothing but ideology and mythology, or at the very least that it does not fit in with the everyday experience of the ordinary Christian. For this reason I would like to set out in what follows a few indications of how we actually encounter the gift of piety in our lives and how it can become something that can be experienced by every Christian who is ready to commit himself or herself to it.

The gift of the Spirit is Jesus Christ himself. In him God's goodness and benevolence toward humanity has actually appeared to us: in him, in his words and deeds, in his life and death, and in his resurrection what is actually meant by life lived on the basis of grace has become visible to us. Hence he is the lasting foundation and lasting measure of all Christian piety. Scripture calls Jesus Christ "the mystery of piety" (1 Tim. 3:16: "the mystery of our religion" RSV). Christian piety thus means listening to Jesus' words, watching his behavior, continually contemplating and bringing to mind his life and death. This is not meant in the sense of a desperate effort at imitation but in the sense of living from the spirit of Christ, which is the spirit of freedom. The spirit of Jesus Christ continually provides a fresh representation of Jesus Christ as corresponds to the demand of the current situation. The gift of the Spirit thus consists in actual fact of becoming aware of Jesus Christ, allowing oneself to be inspired by him, becoming inwardly filled with him, so as to be able genuinely to live, pray, and work in him and from him. The future of Christianity in our society will primarily depend on men and women who are ready to commit themselves to following Jesus in this radical and uncompromising way.

Normally Jesus Christ encounters us by means of our encountering other men and women, concretely by means of the community of those who believe, the church. According to scripture the church is the normal place where the Spirit is at work; it is his gift and his fruit. There is no question but that this ecclesial dimension of piety keeps us busy today. For many people the church has lost all credibility: they say, "Jesus, yes; the church, no." We cannot analyze in detail here the many different reasons that have led to this attitude. But even without such an analysis we can say that this suspicion and distrust has its reasons. But we would also have reason to distrust ourselves and our subjective piety. It is precisely piety threatened in this way that needs a certain objectivity to make it independent of personal moods and emotions. It needs stimulation and criticism from outside. It needs above all the fruitful stimulus of the great treasury of traditional Christian spirituality. Not least it needs the community, not just the small comprehensible group but, today in particular, the world-wide solidarity of all believers. It is in the sharing and application in this way of the very different gifts of the Spirit that Paul sees the Spirit of Christ at work. The church for him therefore is not some dead inflexible system but an event, a process. The high point of Christian piety with this kind of ecclesial dimension is the common celebration of the Eucharist. In this the gift of the Spirit is granted us in its solidest reality. Perhaps it is now more understandable why readiness to take one's place in the community of the church is regarded by the New Testament as an important indication of the genuineness of one's piety and why disunity, dissension, and resentment count as signs of a false spirituality (cf. Rom. 12:4 ff., 1 Cor. 12:4 ff.). This kind of churchmanship need not and cannot remain uncritical with regard to ossification and fossilization, or with regard to established patterns of compromise: quite the contrary. But it will also be grateful for everything for which it is indebted to the larger community of the church, above all for its transmission of the message of Jesus Christ to us.

Finally, the gifts of the Spirit are allotted to every individual personally. According to scripture everyone has his or her gift of the Spirit, his or her charism, and his or her mission. The gift of piety must therefore be something that can be experienced in the everyday life of every Christian. There is in fact something like a mysticism of Christian everyday life. Perhaps it is not to any very great extent the subject of conscious reflection, remaining undeveloped and hidden anonymously beneath the experiences of everyday life. But if we only open ourselves a little to them we discern even in the humdrum things and experiences of everyday life signs that point us toward a deeper, inexpressible mystery of our existence: we experience inward encouragement toward what is good and warning against evil. The pious person is one who is ready to commit himself or herself to this guidance of the Spirit and surrender to it. Scripture calls the children of God those who let themselves be led by the Spirit (cf. Rom. 8:14). According to the theologians the charism of piety consists of a special sensitivity for the guidance of the Spirit and a docile readiness to be led by him. It can lead us on quite unexpected and very different paths. There are many different forms of piety according to one's capabilities, circumstances, sex, civilization, and epoch. Each must find his or her own way. Common to all these different ways is that one must be ready to entrust oneself to the impulse of the Spirit and to allow him room to work.

Being a Christian by entrusting oneself to the guidance of the Spirit is therefore not some rigid and inflexible stance but a way, a journey. And on one's journey one has also to make one's farewells. Sensitivity to the guidance of the Spirit includes sensitivity for when certain forms of spirituality, which were quite right and fruitful in the past, have reached their end and must give way to new forms. This dimension of time and history has not been very developed in our traditional piety. Often people have clung exclusively to the experiences of the past and thus sinned against the present and the future. People's ideas of the working of the Spirit have somehow or other lacked imagination. But it is precisely the pious man or woman who believes in the present and future of the Spirit who must have courage and confidence for what is new and thus become a sign of hope for others. It is not the patina of being old-fashioned but the atmosphere of hope that must distinguish Christian piety and spirituality.

Four

THE CHURCH AND THE CLAIMS OF THE FUTURE

I

"God is dead!" "What are these churches then, if they are not the tombs and graves of God?" That was the diagnosis and prophecy of Friedrich Nietzsche toward the end of the last century, and today it must be many peoples' conviction. It is of course not the first time the church has been declared dead. In the centuries when it was persecuted by the Roman Empire it had, humanly speaking, few chances of survival; in the tenth century, it was called the *saeculum obscurum;* in the later middle ages it was morally at an end; and it was socially and politically at an end after the wave of secularization at the beginning of the nineteenth century. At that time its external structures had almost totally collapsed; Pope Pius VI was deported by the troops of the newly founded French Republic and died a prisoner at Valence in 1799. Shortly before one of the Republic's Directors had written, "This old idol will be destroyed. That is the wish of freedom and of philosophy. . . . What is wanted is for Pius VI to remain alive for two more years so that philosophy will have time to complete its work and leave this lama of Europe without a successor."

None of the many funeral orations pronounced over the papacy and the church have turned out to be true. Each nadir was followed by a peak of religious and theological renewal. Again and again a future has been bestowed on the church. Even the process of secularization was seen in the long view to be an overdue liberation from historical ballast. Soon afterward, in Vienna, Münster, Mainz, and not least in the Catholic Tübingen school, there emerged a renewal of the church the effects of which continued into our own century and which received its official confirmation from the Second Vatican Council. Meanwhile the revolutionary mood of the Council has been followed by a profound depression. Many people no longer believe in the future of the church. In many countries in eastern Europe and in the Third World a persecution is under way that exceeds that of the first centuries of the church's history. There may indeed be little open hostility to the church in the western world, but it is regarded more as the outdated relic of a past epoch. The indifference the church encounters here can be more deadly than direct persecution. The drive toward a more subjective approach and the question of meaningfulness that has once again become acute have so far not had the effect of greater commitment toward and within the church.

As far as the church is concerned the question of the future arises in a new form. There are external and internal reasons for this. The external reasons are to be found in the unprecedented extent of the challenge the future poses both to our society and to the church. At the moment the church is in a process of transition from the European and North American context, in which it has hitherto operated, into the Third World. In the year 2000 some two-thirds of all Catholics will be living in the Third World, so people are already talking today of the Third Church. It is clear that this kind of shift of geographical emphasis will also make a reorientation necessary in the realm of ideas.

Even in Europe the church today encounters a new situation. In the past it was relatively easy for the church to take an unambiguous and therefore convincing stand. Either it became involved in the prevailing social and cultural system and penetrated it from within, or it decisively rejected it and risked persecution. Both options were clear and unambiguous. Today the difficulty for the church in deciding what kind of a stance to adopt lies in the fact that society no longer presents a clear and unambiguous picture with sharp outlines. The contemporary western world somehow lacks definition. There are no great dominant images, goals, and perspectives. All the old values have become subjects for inquiry, and an enormous question mark is attached to all the ideals of the past. A ghastly void has opened behind an apparently sound facade. This lack of meaning is not just a personal problem but a political one too. The roots of terrorism are to be found here.

This is precisely the situation that Nietzsche had already predicted as the consequence of his message of the death of God. The horizon has been wiped away as if with an enormous sponge, he said. There is no longer an above and a below, and we wander around lost "as in an infinite nothing." The nihilism this raises means the devaluation of the supreme values. There is no answer to the questions why or what for. All values and truths are merely estimations, perspectives, and interests that are judged according to whether they encourage and sustain life. Survival is the only perspective. But what is the point of living? Has living any meaning at all? The immediacy and relevance of the problems Nietzsche raised is quite clear. In many ways his views strike me as being more immediately relevant than those of Karl Marx, which over the last ten years many have seen as the challenge to the church. My own view is that Nietzsche defined the situation in which the church stands today and in which its future is being decided more clearly than any other thinker.

It is not just the questions Nietzsche raised that are immediately topical. The answers he tried to give are more topical than people usually realize. Nietzsche's most precipitous idea is that of the eternal recurrence of the same, an idea that suddenly came to him when walking in the Engadine. His aim is to overcome nihilism by accepting the divided nature of existence circling in on itself and indeed by addressing man as a being that rises and falls. This is none other than the renewal of the old myth of the periodic creation and destruction of the universe, of the cosmos that is born from chaos and sinks back into chaos, of the eternal battle of the gods. A similar diagnosis was offered by the great sociologist Max Weber only a little later. He saw the return of polytheism in modern pluralism, in which the world's various different value systems are locked in inextricable combat with each other: "The multitude of old gods, stripped of their magic powers and thus appearing in the guise of impersonal forces, arise from their graves, strive to exert mastery over our life and begin again their eternal battle with each other."

The relativism and pluralism of the contemporary world therefore represents not progress but the return of mythological patterns of thought. This makes the challenge the church encounters in the contemporary world much clearer and more unambiguous than at first appeared. Today there seems to be a recurrence in a new form of the disputes and debates that had to be endured with myth in the early parts of the Bible and with gnosticism at the beginning of the church's history. What is involved is not marginal questions of belief but rather the fundamental question concerning the totality of God, the world, and humankind. It is the question of meaning or absurdity, of the possibility of truth and a system of values. It is not fortuitous that the Bible begins with the division of the primeval chaos into an above and a below, into light and darkness. It ends with the last judgment and the victory of good over evil, of justice over injustice, of life over death. The order and organization of the world is based on the distinction between yes and no. Allowing yes to be no yes and no to be no no comes from the devil: he is the *diabolos,* the power of chaos in the world willed by God.

In the present situation of general relativism and indifference the church must first make fundamental distinctions clear again and encourage decision. But it can only do this if it is itself once again a determined and decisive church with the courage to make distinctions. If in our society the church actually wants a future, then it must first of all consider itself. Only in this way can it be perceived once again as a challenging alternative to a reality that, to a considerable extent, has been drained of meaning; only in this way can it develop new power to enlighten. What then is the specific nature of Christian hope in the future?

II

When Nietzsche was writing about the death of God and about the churches as the tombs and graves of God, his friend, the historian and theologian Franz Overbeck, was rediscovering the focus and perspective of Jesus' message: the imminent approach of the kingdom of God that brings everything that is of the world to a crisis and means a comprehensive re-creation. In his gospel Mark summarizes the whole of Jesus' message in the saying "The time is fulfilled, and the kingdom of God is at hand" (1:15). From this Jesus deduces the need for conversion and a definite reorientation in faith.

Other people, notably Albert Schweitzer and Johannes Weiss, took up this discovery of Overbeck's. As a consequence the future became, in a variety of different forms, the central subject of twentieth-century theology. This led to a rediscovery of what is specific and distinctive in Christianity: not the old song of the eternal recurrence of the same but the category of the new; not a cyclic view of nature turning in on itself but history directed toward a specific goal and open to the future. There was a fresh awareness that the Christian God is a God who leads people along the way, a God of hope and of history. He is not both yes and no at one and the same time; rather, in Jesus Christ he is the final and definitive yes to all promises.

The Second Vatican Council discussed this subject. In his memorable opening speech Pope John saw humankind entering on a new epoch and a day of radiant sunshine dawning in the church. The Council defined the church as the messianic people on pilgrimage in history, making its way through time surrounded by hope and fear, joy and sadness. Karl Rahner then defined Christianity as the religion of the absolute future. Subsequently the theology of the future became of particular importance in connection with the debate with neo-Marxism, especially with the utopian ideas of Ernst Bloch. Giving an account of the hope that is in us has become a central subject of statements of principle by synods and by assemblies of the World Council of Churches. All the churches are beginning to understand themselves more and more as the sacrament of the future.

There is thus an essential link between the church and the future. The claim of the future is not just something that reaches the church from outside: it springs from what is most specifically its own concern—Jesus' messsage of the coming kingdom of

God. Hence the claim of the future affects the church itself. It can only offer the world hope for the future if it is itself open to the future, if it lives from the power of hope, and if it continually enters on the venture of what is new. The church itself must live on the basis of the conviction that God is present in every moment of history.

The revolution brought about by the Council and the figure of John XXIII were testimony of this kind of hope. In recent years many promising beginnings have remained bogged down. There is the change in ecumenical relations, the reform of canon law, particularly of marriage law, and much else besides. But the danger exists in the church at present of making fear rather than hope one's counselor, of adopting a purely defensive stance, or of relying on petty maneuvers that obscure the truth just as much as do superficial publications that evacuate the faith. The fatal element in this kind of faint-hearted reaction is that it is basically only a reflection of the lack of perspective and hope in our society. It is precisely a church that draws in its horns that adapts itself to Nietzsche's proclamation of the death of God, whereas a church open to the future takes up the challenge this contains. For to say that God is dead does not mean that he does not exist at all but that no life proceeds from him, that he does not get anything moving and, therefore, has no future. Only a living church can bear witness to the living God.

In contrast to the enthusiasm generated during and immediately after the Council, today we can perhaps see more clearly that this kind of openness to the future does not mean some kind of pop Christianity to which public opinion belongs. Rather we know that a genuinely Christian openness to the future leads to conflicts of which we are seeing only the first indications today.

It is not a question of any kind of future and of an arbitrary openness to everything and anything. It is rather a question of a quite definite future, the future of God in Jesus Christ. According to Jesus this demands a clear and unequivocal decision: it is only possible through a process of conversion. God shows himself to be living by getting something moving in the depths of man's being. Alternatively we can say quite bluntly that according to Jesus the future is only promised to the person who repents—who, as Paul says, does not conform himself or herself to this world but reforms his or her thinking and discovers the will of God. But in the contemporary church nothing is at a lower ebb than the spirit and practice of repentance. When readiness to be transformed inwardly fades and dies and is at best replaced by outward reforms, when the courage to decide and distinguish is lacking, then there is a failure to recognize what Jesus' idea of the future is all about; then the church is dead. Nietzsche saw these connections very clearly, and in his hostility to Christianity did not discredit anything so much as the cross.

Let us therefore ask how a church must look that wants to do justice to the claim of the future coming of the kingdom of God.

III

The future the church has to talk about and bear witness to through its life is first of all God's future: "For I know the plans I have for you, . . . to give you a future and a hope," the prophet Jeremiah has God say in a letter to the exiles in Babylon. God alone is meant and none other beside or even against him. That is the entire message of the Old Testament and the anticipation of the New. What therefore is involved in Christianity is not the future that we plan, make, and shape: this future would merely be an extension of the world in which we are living and at best would involve merely relatively minor improvements at a time when we are aware that every progress entails a regress and creates fresh problems. But above all our real problems cannot be overcome in this way: the necessity of dying, the longing for absolute justice, in a word, hope for life.

If the church bears witness to the future that God alone grants, then it comes into conflict with that image of man emptied of all mystery that sees humans simply as beings of instinctive impulses and needs and that rejects all hunger for meaning and thirst for justice for the living and the dead as false consciousness and a vain promise of consolation. A church that talks of hope in God must therefore resist total adaptation to a society built on this kind of principle. It must point to the deeper sources of human life. In our society based on achievement this means the church comes into conflict with those utopias that strive to create this future by their own efforts. Thinking in this highpowered way in terms of achievement turns men and women into the slaves of plans and programs: it cuts hope in two in favor of those who are in the vanguard of progress and forgets the underdogs and those who suffer in the past and in the present. With its message of God the church recalls not only human greatness but also human misery, powerlessness, and finite nature. It is precisely in this way that it does justice to humanity as a whole.

A church dominated by the claim of God's future will therefore be a church that takes seriously what is its original and proper task—bearing witness to God. Hence it will primarily be a church that sees its most important task as celebrating the worship of God. By this means it will also measure up to its responsibility for the future of humanity. Feast and celebration, praise and thanksgiving, the acknowledgement of guilt and the proclamation of forgiveness are profoundly human and humanizing things. They belong to our humanity. They are the answers to our alienation by means of mere adaptation to our needs and by means of the excessive demands placed on us by thinking purely in terms of achievement. Only when humans point toward an ultimate mystery that is apart from themselves and from everyone else can their dignity as humans be safeguarded. Respect for God and respect for humanity belong together. The church as the community assembled in worship therefore escapes the unstable dilemma of putting all its trust in the other world or concentrating exclusively on this world, between being guided by the gospel and being guided by contemporary expectations, between being resolute for God and open for humanity. It is precisely as a church totally committed to God that it will also be a completely human church, a house with a welcome for all.

The claim of the future under which the church stands is secondly the future of Jesus Christ. The conviction of Christian faith is that God's future has already begun in the death and resurrection of Jesus Christ. Hence he is the lasting foundation, the visible form, and the enduring measure of the future that the church has to proclaim and itself to bring about. But what kind of a future is it that Jesus Christ proclaims? A clear answer is given by the beatitudes of the Sermon on the Mount. Jesus there calls blessed those who are poor, those who mourn and are battered, those who are pure and simple in heart, those who suffer, who are persecuted and oppressed. It is no accident that Jesus himself went the way of the cross. The future that is revealed on the cross is not simply progress in a straight line, the evolution of what already exists. The future of him who was crucified is a crucified future: it is the future of new life in the power of resurrection from the dead.

The church living under the claim of the future will therefore have to begin by summoning itself to follow Jesus and become his disciple. What this means in practical terms is that the church must more clearly and more decisively become an institution of freedom in love. Following Jesus Christ—in other words, taking him as our standard—sets us free from prejudices and idols, from the anxiety about self-preservation that often enough devours us inwardly, from ourselves, in order to serve others selflessly. A mature Christian, according to the Bible, is someone who does not let himself or herself be led astray and subjugated by the wisdom of the world, but who rather clings to the folly of the cross, who knows the rudiments of Christian doctrine, and does not let himself or herself be blown about by every wind of opinion.

This kind of Christian freedom creates the prerequisite for the church to open itself in the future to a greater extent and more decisively than hitherto to the history of freedom in modern times, something which indeed for its part has Jesus' message of freedom to thank for its motivation, and for it to open the way to procedures of freedom within the church in a less half-hearted and hesitant manner. The excess of regimentation and bureaucracy in the contemporary church very often buries the freedom of the children of God and makes the idea of creative love wither away: the church's excessively bureaucratic form of organization creates institutional pressures that stifle hope.

But it would be to misunderstand the freedom for which Jesus Christ set us free if one were to understand it in a one-sidedly individualistic and private manner. Christian freedom is freedom from oneself in order to be free for others. Today, especially, it is in this selfless service that following Christ in discipleship has to prove itself. A particularly urgent reminder of this task comes from the Third Church and the prevailing situation there of poverty and oppression. In the German Synod's document *Our Hope* we read, "We shall survive our intellectual doubters more easily than the inarticulate doubts of the poor and insignificant and their memory of the church's failure." It is precisely a community assembled for worship that must not exclude from its fellowship the many who have no bread. Here it is a question of paying the price of our catholicity. Otherwise the religion of the cross is turned into a bourgeoisified religion of well-being.

The third and final point is that the power and the strength of God's future is, as scripture bears witness, the Spirit of God. According to Romans 8 God accepts the longing and expectation of the tormented creature and leads it toward the realm of freedom it hopes for. It is not only within the walls of the church that the Spirit blows: rather, he is at work everywhere in the world and in its history where men and women hunger and thirst after righteousness, where they break through the shell of egosim and commit themselves to God and their neighbor. He ultimately and finally broke through in Jesus Christ and continues Christ's work in history. Hence the church will have a future when and where it is totally open to this Spirit of Jesus Christ. The future of the church will be determined by the men and women who let themselves be driven by the Spirit of God: it will be a church that is spiritually renewed.

But what do spirit and spiritual life mean? For the Bible the spirit is not just something inward and internal. The opposite to spirit in scripture is not the body but the flesh, in other words, life on the basis of what is visible, verifiable, calculable, and manipulable, as opposed to life on the basis of belief in God and his hidden working. Hence a spiritual man or woman and a spiritually renewed church are a man or woman or a church that lives from the power of faith, hope, and love, from the power of prayer and sacrifice.

What, on the other hand, makes the church appear so unworthy of belief to so many today is the fact that, because of its history, it has become involved in the systems and interests of our social life in so many different ways and is continually trying to establish itself in the world so as to retain positions and privileges that have become questionable as a result of the historical situation and even more on the basis of the gospel. Christendom has fallen away from Christianity, remarked one of Nietzsche's great contemporaries, Søren Kierkegaard, and in this he coincides with the verdict of Nietzsche's friend Franz Overbeck, for whom Jesus' message of the kingdom of God seemed irreconcilable with a Christianity expressed in terms of secular culture. Both verdicts echo a devaluation of the reality of the visible creation, and this is not very biblical. But what is right about both of them is that the church's path into the future is not the path of liberal interpretation but rather the path of radically taking the gospel seriously.

Hence a church of the future will in many things be simpler and more unpretentious. It will perhaps be a diaspora church throughout the world, as when it began. Our parishes will then once again look like the settlements of strangers in exile, as is suggested by the biblical term *paroikia*, from which our term derives. The great basilicas and cathedrals of the past will then seem too large, perhaps also too rich and too powerful. Nevertheless these cathedrals will be more than the graves and tombs of God if the congregations that gather in them to worship God are spiritually alive. If they grow inwardly, the witness of the few will convince the many of the power of Christian hope more than the external facade of popular Christianity and a church of the people.

No one can know whether it will be so or or how precisely it will turn out. There is only one thing we do know from both the Bible and history: the future of the church will be determined by the saints, by the holy men and women who open themselves completely to the working of the spirit. They are witnesses to the God who is not dead but alive and is continually reawakening life in the church in astonishing and unexpected ways. Hence one of the most hopeful signs of renewal in the church are the movements of spiritual renewal emerging everywhere in many different forms. If they did not exist, then the church would deserve to be thrown out like salt that has lost its savor. But it is in this way too that it should in the contemporary world bear witness to and give an account of the hope that is in it.

Five

THE PRIEST'S NATURE AND MISSION
Thoughts on the Future of the Priestly Ministry

The present situation

In the subject of this essay we encounter, separated out as in a prism, pretty well all the problems with which we have had to battle over the last two decades. There is the enormous cultural and social change that has radically altered the priest's position and status. There is the new awareness in the fields of biblical theology and the history of dogma that began by shaking for many the traditional dogmatic image of the priest but went on fundamentally to enrich it. There is the new awareness brought about by the Council of the church's nature and mission in the world today and the renewal of the common priesthood of all the baptized, a renewal temporarily misunderstood as a democratization of the church but which in the long run has led to new forms of the coresponsibility of the laity in the pastoral ministry and to a comprehensive change in the forms and styles of pastoral work. There are the recent discussions in christology, since the debates about a christology "from above" or "from below" obviously cannot be without profound effects on our understanding of the church and the priestly ministry. There is finally the discussion about the question of God which for the past fifteen years at least has represented the basic drift of theological debate.

Over the past two decades all these debates and discussions were in part accompanied by elements of crisis. I need recall only my brethren in the priesthood who have resigned from their ministry. But nothing indicates the desperate straits we are in more clearly than what until recently has been a catastrophic decline in the number of candidates for the priesthood. Everyone is aware of what virtually insoluble problems arise from this development both today and to a greater extent in the near future for the pastoral ministry in our congregations.

The subject

It is obviously impossible to tackle all these complex problems adequately in the space available. What follows can therefore only be a very modest contribution, that of a theologian. It is his task to set out the fundamental questions. What really is priestly ministry? For what do we need priests? What brings us into the priestly ministry and keeps us there? With questions like these the theologian will energetically combat all superficial attempts at a solution that claims to be able to solve the existing problems merely by organizational means. That our Christian communities should be alive is more necessary than all the possible and doubtless also essential forms of activity. Our communities will only be living communities if we reflect anew on the origins and sources of human and Christian life. At a time when the questions that are asked about the church's ministry are virtually restricted to when, who, and how but hardly ever what, when we are in danger of forgetting the factual issues through concentrating purely on questions of method, the theologian will once again raise this question about the factual basis of the priestly ministry. Only consideration of the sources, of the gospel of Jesus Christ, can lead to a genuine renewal. In making this attempt I would like to take as my starting point a sentence from the First Letter to the Corinthians: "This is how one should regard us, as servants of Christ and stewards of the mysteries of God" (4:1). One could hardly describe the priest's nature and mission more precisely. I would therefore like to try to elucidate this saying of Paul's in three sections.

The Priest as Man of God

A *sober look at the situation*
If one wants to speak in appropriate terms of the priest as the steward of God's mysteries, then the first essential is to see the situation in which this takes place, plain and unadorned. Among the most serious aspects of our age is the message that God is dead. This does not exclude most people in our society keeping some kind of idea of God in some hidden corner of their heart and bringing it to life as occasion offers. Nor does it exclude people, particularly the young, sensing the lack of meaning in a society geared to efficiency and consumption and looking for new forms of meditation and new ways of experiencing meaning and transcendence. Above all it does not exclude the existence, today as formerly, of a large number of serious religious-minded people who strive to let their faith shape their lives. But public awareness and the standards publicly recognized as valid are less and less marked by these forms of religious feeling that still exist. To say that God is dead does not mean that he does not exist in any way but that no life proceeds from him and that many people experience this death of God precisely as a liberation from previous restrictions on their ideas and their behavior. To this extent mass atheism must be counted among the signs of the times.

It is primarily this situation that makes the priest's ministry so difficult today. As soon as he leaves his shrunken flock he encounters a very tenuous atmosphere that easily makes him catch his breath. As a result many priests feel themselves to be like the taillight of a train that long since seems to have passed by in quite a different direction. They have the impression of no longer belonging, as if a new world were being made that no longer had any need of them. The consequence is often resignation, defeatism, or aggressiveness. A process that began in the age of the Enlightenment has now reached its full effect on the masses. I do not think we can look forward to a fundamental

change of tendency. This situation must be looked at with courage. It is no use complaining or making accusations, less still
hurling reproaches at each other.

Judging on the basis of Christian faith
Seeing the situation must lead on to judging as the second step.
The criterion for judgment can only be Christian faith. The
conviction of our faith is that God is our origin and goal. Because
of our nature as creatures we cannot shake loose of God even
if we wanted to. As long as humans live God cannot be dead for
them because at every moment he must unceasingly keep them
alive if they are not to sink back into nothingness. Whenever
men and women commit themselves to the ground of their being,
when they drop all the masks worn for outward show and accept
the dark mystery of their lives in a hope that is perhaps defiant
but perhaps also patient, when they break with routine, forgive
one another, are present for one another in selfless love and
loyalty, then they necessarily touch on the mystery of God even
if in a perhaps concealed manner. Perhaps it is merely our fault
that we have not yet discovered the new ways in which contemporary men and women experience God or that we are not yet
able to provide an adequate formulation of them. If this kind
of experience no longer existed today in any form, then humans
would have bred themselves back to being merely resourceful
animals, for the mystery of God is the ultimate foundation of
the mystery of humanity. Only if humans project into an ultimate
mystery that is distinct from themselves do they have a dignity
that is not at their own or others' disposal. Today one can offer
something like a negative proof of this thesis. With the loss of
the dimension of religious mystery the sense of man's inviolable
dignity is also disappearing. People start manipulating people,
their births as well as their deaths. It is no accident that the
demand is heard today for the western myth of man to be reduced to ashes and the traditional European idea of human
dignity to be buried. Hence for the sake of humanity we cannot
and must not cease in the future to talk of God and bear witness
to his reality. We shall have to say much more clearly than hitherto that turning to God and a new respect for and awe of God

are the only possible ways toward a more human way of being human and toward a society more in keeping with human dignity.

Acting as a priest

Acting follows from seeing and judging. It is a generally accepted finding of social history and the history of religion that every society needs institutions of transcendence. Their job is to provide a public symbolic representation of the dimension of the divine that embraces everything and gives it unity and meaning and, as it were, to articulate verbally and still more symbolically the fundamental consensus without which a society cannot live. The attempt to build a society on an atheistical foundation or on one indifferent in matters of religion is still very recent in terms of historical perspective: it is barely a century old and has not in any way yet passed the test of historical verification. Quite the contrary: despite all prophecies of an imminent end of religion on account of the progress of secularization, we must acknowledge today that the need for religion cannot be brought to disappearing-point and indeed that it is coming to life again precisely where for decades the attempt has been made to suppress it by force.

It is only religion that is capable of giving life a meaning in the face of evils like guilt and death that cannot be ovecome by science and politics. Admittedly we must criticize the false consolation created by putting one's trust in another world in cases where aid and assistance are available in terms of this world: when the other world becomes merely a means of providing consolation then this world is robbed of consolation. Who then would console those whom with the best will in the world we are unable to console, who would console those long since dead who are no longer able to participate in the world of freedom for which they strove, who would console the victims and failures of history, who finally would console the privileged in the face of humankind's inescapable suffering? In the face of such questions there has been agreement up till now that the office of pontiff is needed, and it is not remotely evident who could otherwise take this function over in our society, or what other source there could be for the possibility of universal meaning than religion and those who are its representatives.

Institutions of transcendence of this kind are very much under threat, not so much from without as from within. They are continually in danger of confusing themselves with the cause they represent. Christianity is not immune from this danger. In fact, looking at its history, it has every reason to be critical of itself, a kind of self-criticism particularly suitable for Christianity. Only in a very critical manner has it taken up the phenomenon of priesthood that is universal in the history of religion. This is shown by the very terminology used by the Bible. It keeps the title of priest for the one high priest Jesus Christ. He accomplishes his priesthood on the cross: he directs us to God while radically emptying himself so as to be totally a sign and a void for God. The cross is therefore the basic image and the permanent norm of Christian priesthood.

This cannot be without its consequences for the way in which we have to make present this priesthood of Jesus Christ. By its very nature the priesthood of the New Testament cannot be a sign and institution of transcendence on the basis of outward respect or worldly domination. The priest is God's sign and witness in the world primarily by entering totally into the mode of Jesus' being on the cross. The priest, whose job it is to be a steward of the mystery of God, must therefore be first of all a man of faith. By this we mean not only accepting correctly doctrinal formulations, but also faith in the more comprehensive biblical sense of building on and trusting in God, of taking one's stand on what one does not see, of a life that finds it certainty and its standards not in the available certainties but that draws its strength from hope in what one cannot create and plan oneself. This kind of faith is expressed above all in prayer. The first task of the priest is therefore to glorify God, to worship God. It is precisely the celebration of the Eucharist that expresses the fact that ultimately we do not live on the basis of what we can achieve ourselves but that we owe our lives and their fulfillment to God. What is expressed here is that being human cannot be reduced to work and achievement, not to consumption or protest, but finds its fulfillment in feast and celebration. This may not be a very profound remark from the point of view of the critique of society, but today it is a very necessary one. There cannot be anything more human than celebrating a service of worship.

This has nothing to do with reducing religion to individual consolation. The political dimension of religion and therefore of the priest cannot in any way be disputed. But the political dimension lies within the dimension of the religious itself: it is not something that springs from external political stances and campaigns. No one disputes the importance of this kind of social and political commitment, but for this alone there is no need of the church nor of the priest. The social relevance of the church, and above all of the priest, does not arise from repeating in different and somewhat loftier terms what many others are already saying and have for the most part been saying sooner and better than we. What makes the priest socially relevant is above all that he performs his specific ministry that no one else can do. Talking of God is the form of political service or *diakonia* that is proper to the priest. Precisely as a man of faith and a man of prayer he can be a light and strength for lay people for the service they are charged with carrying out in the world. What is true of the priest therefore is that he is appointed for men and women but in their business with God. Today this ministry is the one thing necessary.

The Priest as the Servant of Jesus Christ

The mystery of God that the priest has to serve is hidden from us. At best we can only catch a glimpse of it. This is not something that has only just begun to be the case but has fundamentally and always been so. Hence the priest seems to have an impossible job. But the core of the Christian message holds that this incomprehensible mystery of God has become comprehensible in Jesus Christ, the immeasurable God became measurable in him in space and time, the invisible visible, the distant present, that the eternal silence became audible in our world. In many places scripture speaks of the mystery of God hidden from all eternity but made manifest in history in Jesus Christ. It adds that in the mystery of God the mystery of man has also finally been made manifest. Hence it describes Jesus Christ both as the son of God from all eternity and as the new Adam.

The christological basis of the priestly ministry

Jesus Christ, true God and true man: this is the fundamental truth of our faith and includes all the others and also discloses the priest's mission. Here we cannot go into the large-scale discussion of christology that in contemporary theology is centered around this fundamental truth. Nevertheless one thing must be clear to us: if Jesus Christ were only a man and nothing other than a man, then all he could give us would be only human, then we would not be redeemed by him in our specific distress, in the distress of our sin, in the distress of dying, and in the distress of our finiteness. Only God can save us from death. But if Jesus Christ were not also true and complete man, like us in all things bar sin alone, then God could not reach us through him in our humanness, then salvation would remain abstract, empty, and hollow. It is only the entire Jesus Christ, the Jesus of history and the Christ of faith, who can be the ground of our hope. The entire Jesus Christ is the mystery to which we must bear witness. Anyone who undermines this or even merely evades the issue is undermining the foundations of being a Christian and obscuring what gives Christianity its specific power of illumination.

Jesus Christ, the one mediator between God and man, is at the same time the one and only priest of the new covenant. All other priesthood can only be a sharing in his priesthood. Today we are more clearly aware than formerly that this sharing in the priesthood of Jesus Christ belongs to all who have been baptized and confirmed. All together form the one priestly people of God in which there must be many different gifts. But this joint sharing in the one priesthood of Jesus Christ is not something that one simply "has" or can rely on: it is something that is given to us and must continually be imparted to us anew. This is where the task of the special priesthood lies. Following a phrase in the letter to the Ephesians, it serves "the equipment of the saints for the work of ministry" (4:12). It is a ministry directed to other ministries, a ministry exercised in the power of Jesus Christ. The priest must equip his congregation for their ministry by making Jesus Christ present as their foundation and their standard.

By the laying on of hands and prayer, the sacrament of ordination bestows its essential element, a specific equality with Jesus Christ, and thereby constitutes the one ordained to be a public and official witness of Jesus Christ in ministry to the other ministries. Once and for all it enables the priest to speak and act in the name of Jesus Christ. Properly understood this does not justify any claim to clerical power. Speaking and acting in the name of Jesus Christ also means speaking and acting in the way Jesus Christ did, making him present not only by official acts but through the witness of one's life.

Here we touch on the specific mystery of the priestly ministry. As the authorized servant of Jesus Christ the priest must at the same time be the friend of Jesus Christ: "No longer do I call you servants, for the servant does not know what his master is doing; but I have called you friends, for all that I have heard from my Father I have made known to you" (John 15:15). Friendship with Jesus Christ should be the most profound and ultimate motive that gives one courage to become a priest and supports one through life as a priest. This friendship with Jesus Christ also provides the key to solve one of the most difficult problems with which many priests see themselves faced today. They find themselves in a crisis because they have the impression that their ministry is splintered into an almost intolerable abundance of duties and tasks which continually threaten to become more than they can handle. The life of the priest can only attain a sense of identity if it is oriented by its essential core, if it obtains a uniform line from Jesus Christ, and if it has a center of gravity in community and friendship with him. Let us therefore try to describe the ministry of the priest for Jesus Christ a little more precisely under three heads, even if it can only be a question of very fragmentary indications.

Threefold exposition of the priestly ministry
(1) Jesus Christ is God's final and definitive word that can bring meaning, direction, and perspective into our lives. Hence the ministry of the priest for Jesus Christ is first of all ministry of

the word. This means something very comprehensive and all-embracing: not just preaching but also conversation; not just the prepared address but also the casual remark, the greeting; not just the spoken but also the sung word, psalms and hymns and spiritual songs. Throughout, however, the focus is on one thing: we preach Christ crucified. The content of our proclamation must be not our own thoughts and expectations, nor the half-understood content of the last article we happen to have read, but the gospel of Jesus Christ as this is testified by scripture and transmitted by the tradition of the church.

There is no doubt that this gospel must be addressed to the man and woman of today. This does not mean indoctrination by the repetition of formulae on which one draws as on preserves in the larder. What is involved is the living gospel that throws light on the actual conditions of life and enters into practical details. The man or woman of today is therefore the goal of our proclamation of the gospel, but he or she is not its criterion. The gospel has something to say to him or her, and indeed something decisive, unique, irreplaceable, and insurpassable: it has its pre-scribed content in Jesus Christ. Hence we must not trim the message to fit in with what seems right and proper today: rather we should explode the fashionable plausibilities of the day for the sake of humanity in order to direct it toward the greater hope, the greater fulfillment, and the greater joy that await.

The ministry of the word of God is therefore a process of translation that can only succeed if first of all we have translated the Christian message into our own life. Proclamation does indeed mean *contemplata tradere*, handing on the fruits of one's own contemplation. Hence as priests we must above all live on the basis of the study and the contemplation of the word of God. Today we are bound to remain amateurs in much that we do. It is impossible for us to be professionals in everything demanded of us, but we must be professionals when it is a question of giving information about faith and its meaning for life. This will not happen without continuous theological effort, and this is where the priority must lie in our present situation of diaspora.

(2) In Jesus Christ the word of God took bodily form. As the word Jesus Christ is therefore also the sacrament; in other words

the incarnate sign and instrument of God in the world. The word of the gospel must therefore continually be embodied in actual symbolic actions. Ministry for Jesus Christ is always also ministry of the sacraments. These sacraments are not magical signs but the embodied word of grace, social embodiments of Christian reconciliation. They accompany human life in all its phases and at all its decisive nodes. Hence the fully fledged ministry of the sacraments is anything but a mere ritual function: it is to the highest degree service toward people. The celebration of the sacraments, especially the celebration of the Eucharist, is therefore the core and summit of the priestly ministry.

The priest's sacramental ministry was in the past often presented in a one-sided and isolated manner. The recent Council put an end to this narrowing down and understood the sacramental ministry on the basis of the proclamation of the word of God and as directed toward the building up of community. This means first of all that the sacraments are only fruitful and meaningful when they actually arouse faith, hope, and love. This spiritual fruit must be our criterion for spiritual renewals. The renewal of the liturgy of the sacraments would be misunderstood if one were to see it as a mere reform of ritual rather than as a reform springing from faith and directed toward living. It was not for nothing that the Council said, "Ceremonies, however excellently performed, and gatherings, however flourishing, are of little use if they are not directed toward the edification of men and women toward Christian maturity." This means secondly that the sacraments do not primarily serve private edification but the building up of community. As the sacraments of the church they are therefore no playground for the subjective piety of the priest who happens to be administering them. The human aspect of the liturgy includes not only what is innovative and experimental but also what is obviously traditional and customary. No one can stand a continual stress on innovation. Tradition and institution are also part of people's heritage. The much abused principle "The sacraments are for people" thus justifies not only breaking away from encrusted traditions but also their creative maintenance as well as the formation of new traditions where people can find themselves at home. Part of the human respect of the liturgy is also that people should feel at home there.

(3) Jesus Christ is not only God's final and definitive word and his eschatological sacrament: he is also the shepherd who goes to look for the lost sheep and gathers those that have been scattered. Ministry for Jesus Christ is therefore the ministry of a shepherd, the ministry of a pastor, and thus pastoral ministry. Jesus' intention was indeed the eschatological assembly of the people of God. On the cross he established peace between God and man and between man and man. Hence the church as the church, formed of Jew and Gentile, the church formed of all peoples and nations, of all classes and races, the anticipation of the eschatological *shalom*, is the sign and instrument of the unity of all humankind. Normally the church takes shape in the local community or congregation. This is not just a segment and administrative subunit of the universal church but the realization and representation of the church in the place where the reality of Christian salvation and Jesus Christ's work of reconciliation are meant to become something actually experienced by the individual Christian. Ministry for Jesus Christ is therefore ministry in the building up of the church and its local communities.

This pastoral ministry is in a special way entrusted to the priest. It is his job to gather communities together, to build them up, and to guide and lead them according to the model of the good shepherd who lays down his life for the sheep. It is his job to make present the unconditional acceptance God offers every man and woman in Jesus Christ by creating in the community a space of brotherhood and sisterhood, a zone of humanity in which everyone is accepted with his or her gifts and responsibilities. It is therefore his job to discover and bring to light individuals' gifts and charisms, to encourage them, to give them room to develop, and to integrate them into a totality. The priest's ministry is the ministry of a shepherd, a pastoral ministry in the root meaning of the word.

If one describes this pastoral ministry as a ministry of leading the community, one means more by this than organization and administration. Leading the community is a spiritual ministry that takes place through the word, through the celebration of the sacraments, and above all through the celebration of the Eucharist as the sacrament of unity. Last but not least this kind of leadership takes place though personal witness: in his concern for humanity God's will is to be present among us by means of human mediation, through the entire life and work of men and women. Pastoral ministry as a disciple following the good shepherd therefore demands the whole human being and requires a specific life-style. To this there belong, on the one hand, simplicity, modesty, unpretentiousness, openness, accessibility, brotherliness, an existence marked by dialogue, an ability to mediate and reconcile, and on the other hand, decisiveness, clarity, lack of equivocation, a willingness to commit oneself and to take responsibility, the gift of leadership.

In summary, to be a priest means to be a pastor.

A solution to the shortage of priests?

This definition of the priest as a pastor makes the extent of the present crisis clear. We all know that we have today and will have in the foreseeable future substantially more parishes than priests to serve them. But a parish without a priest is a contradiction in itself. For the Christian community is essentially defined by the official ministry that equips it for its own ministry. Its center is the celebration of the Eucharist: it is essentially a eucharistic community. But the Eucharist as the sacrament of unity is not possible without the priestly ministry of unity. In this difficult situation we have found many lay people as fellow-workers without whom we would no longer be able to perform our ministry, nor would it be possible for us to do so. The increased responsible cooperation of the laity is among the most positive and satisfactory developments of recent years. Nevertheless these lay fellow-workers are not just a temporary substitute for priests. They have their own mission which will still be necessary when once again we have enough priests. This leads to the conclusion that the shortage of priests can only be overcome by more priests. All efforts at a solution that try to circumvent this essential element do not provide any lasting help. All they do is to magnify the crisis instead of bringing it to an end.

In this context I cannot help asking whether the experiments and plans many dioceses have introduced of services of the word with communion celebrated without a priest have been satisfactorily thought through and solidly established from a theological and pastoral point of view. They do not seem to me to provide a comprehensive and profound enough answer to the desperate pastoral situation. I am of course aware that extraordinary situations do arise when communion apart from the celebration of the Eucharist does make sense. The classic example is the communion of the sick. But has enough thought been given to the consequences if what is right and proper in extraordinary individual cases of this nature is extended to entire communities and made part of their way of life? Has enough thought been given to the consequences that could arise for our understanding of the Christian community, of the church's official ministry, and above all of the Eucharist? Does this not in fact mean retreating from all the new insights into the meaning of the proclamation of the word and of the liturgy of the word as well as from the basic insights of the liturgical movement and its understanding of the Eucharist as an event, retreating from this to an age when communion was regularly distributed before Sunday Mass? I can understand those parishes that have refused to be put off in this way.

I cannot help asking why other solutions are not more openly discussed. If it is agreed that we have enough lay people who are humanly and Christianly competent, which means that they are also theologically competent, to take over in practice the ministry of a parish priest—and this is the presupposition on which the experiments I have mentioned are founded—then I ask myself why such lay people who have proved themselves, and who are therefore *viri probati*, are not made pastors *de iure*, in other words why someone does not lay hands on them and ordain them as priests. This seems to me to be the only logical solution. This question immediately raises a host of other problems. No one can be so naive as to believe that all problems would be solved with the ordination of married men. It is impossible to discuss the entire problem with all its many implications in this context. I shall restrict myself to the basic question. It is not the choice between an unmarried or a married clergy.

It is rather the kind of life that is suitable for the priestly ministry. For if what was said above is correct, if the priest's job is to make Jesus Christ present by his ministry of the word and sacraments and by his pastoral ministry, then this is not something he can do as a mere functionary but something he can only do if he enters into Jesus Christ's way of life, if his life and work are based entirely on the Spirit of Jesus Christ. He must, as it were, become a void to be filled by the Spirit of Jesus Christ who through him makes the person and work of Jesus Christ present here and now in human history. We must now discuss in detail this third aspect of the priestly ministry in the stewardship of the mysteries of God. It will, in my view, provide the key to the present discussion.

The Priest as Mediator of the Spirit

No doubt many will have expected me to talk of the church in this third section after having spoken of God and Jesus Christ. But it would be a strange and novel doctrine of the Trinity if one were to say God—Christ—Church. This would be neo-Platonic speculation rather than a genuinely Christian confession of faith in the Trinity. The church may come in the third place in the Apostles' Creed, but nevertheless it is subordinate to our acknowledgement of belief in the Holy Spirit. The church is merely the place, the area, the sacramental sign through which Jesus Christ in the Holy Spirit is permanently present in history and in the world. The church is therefore not just an organization, not a system, not a religious agency, nor an organization for providing aid for social welfare, not simply an administrative apparatus, and not just an authority. In biblical language it is what God has built in the Holy Spirit; in dogmatic language it is the sacrament of the Spirit. The definition of the church as the sacrament of the Spirit is of fundamental importance for our understanding of the priestly ministry. It means that the priest's ministry as a ministry in and for the church is a spiritual ministry. We shall consider this spiritual dimension of the priestly ministry once again under three heads.

The priest—a spiritual man

The first consequence of the spiritual dimension of the priest-hood is that the priest must be a spiritual man. When he is ordained the Holy Spirit is, through prayer and the laying on of hands, given to him in a special way for his ministry. Indeed, in German the word *Geistlicher*—a spiritual man—means a priest or cleric. But what is a spiritual man? Not simply someone with his head in the clouds. In the Bible there is no question of the Platonic distinction between internal and external, between body and soul. According to the Bible the boundary runs not between what is internal and what is external but between God and human, creator and creature. A spiritual man therefore is someone who does not look on what can be seen, what can be made, what can be planned as the only reality, but makes room for the uncontrollable working of the Spirit of God, someone who lives on the basis of this spiritual element that is not something he can control or dispose of. Living in the Spirit in this way means in actual fact living on the basis of faith, hope, and love, living on the basis of trust in the power of prayer, in the strength of God's word, in the strength that comes from the celebration of the sacraments, and not least living on the basis of faith in the significance of sacrifice, of renunciation, of suffering.

Living a spiritual life on the basis of the hope that springs from faith that in its turn is made effective in love is primarily expressed in living according to the evangelical counsels. Renouncing the security of marriage and family, renouncing the security given by external goods, renouncing outward reputation and external power are symbolic expressions of someone entrusting himself entirely to the reality of the Spirit of God and living on the basis of faith, hope, and love. Living according to the evangelical counsels is therefore a sign of Christian freedom for God and for service to men and women. This kind of spiritual life is to a high degree fitted to the priestly ministry, and the future of the Catholic priesthood will to a decisive extent depend on whether it is successful in arousing more understanding for this way of life once again. It is not misunderstood liberalization but a radical process of taking the gospel seriously that is the way leading to the future.

It is only against this larger background of the spiritual way of life that one can discuss the problem of celibacy adequately. When it is seen in this context there are three things to be said about it. First, voluntary celibacy for the sake of some major venture or cause to which one devotes one's whole existence is a genuine human possibility and does not of itself mean a Manichaean devaluation of marriage and sexuality. Celibacy for the sake of the kingdom of God rests on this natural foundation, even if it adds a whole new series of motives to it. Secondly, voluntary celibacy for the sake of the kingdom of God is a form of life eminently fitted to the priestly ministry. It expresses the lack of security of the person who commits himself to the ministry of the gospel as well as his availability, in other words his freedom for Jesus Christ and for the community. It corresponds to the pattern of existence of Jesus himself, particularly his sacrifice on the cross, which is made present in the Eucharist by the priest's ministry. Thirdly, celibacy is not the only possible expression of the way of life belonging to the priestly ministry. It represents an independent charism or gift distinct from the priestly ministry, and it cannot be proved theologically that it is necessarily and unconditionally bound to the priestly ministry. There is little doubt that the pastoral epistles in the New Testament were issued by married leaders of congregations.

Hence it is not permissible to place at risk such supreme goods as the salvation of Christian communities and the salvation of priests for the sake of something that is valuable but not supremely valuable. This does not mean dismantling what already exists. But part of trusting in the Spirit is being open to being led by the Spirit, something which is indicated in the actual realities of the church. We should therefore pay attention to the multiplicity of the counsels given by the gospel, to the many varied possibilities of a spiritual life, and to the inner coherence of the various evangelical counsels. Celibacy can in fact only be achieved from a human point of view and lived in a way that carries Christian conviction if it is within the context of a spiritual form of life.

What this means in reality is that the celibate form of life for the sake of the gospel needs community and fellowship. Fellow-

ship among priests and the various forms of communities of
priests therefore have great importance today. Young people in
particular are looking for them. Often what they want are credible forms of a spiritual life in keeping with the gospel, forms
that offer an alternative to a late bourgeois civilization that more
and more people are experiencing as hollow and empty. It is
against this background that the form the priest's life should
take needs to be discussed.

I would like to conclude these remarks with a quotation from
Hans Urs von Balthasar: "It is possible that in a future Church
celibate priests will be in the minority. It is possible. It is also
possible that the example of these few will give rise to a new
appreciation of the rightness and indispensability of this form
of life in the Church. It is possible that we must pass through
a time of hunger and thirst but that precisely this lack will arouse
fresh vocations, or rather arouse a fresh generosity in answering
the vocations that are never lacking."

The priest—a man in the world
We must now discuss a second aspect of the spiritual dimension
of the priestly ministry. As a spiritual man the priest must also
at the same time be a worldly man. This may seem a surprising
statement. But according to the Bible the Spirit of God is broader
and greater than the church: he cannot be confined within the
walls of the church but blows where he wills; he is at work everywhere, in the whole of creation and in the whole of history.
According to Romans 8 he can be heard in the whole creation
groaning in travail, and he leads the whole of human history
toward the coming kingdom of freedom. The idea of "anonymous Christians" may not be much use, but what is meant by
the term is incontestable. Hence a spiritual man is bound not
simply to retreat into the quietness of his room but should also
pay attention to the signs of the times and to listen to the strange
prophecies of the world so as to be able to understand the gospel
anew and more profoundly on the basis of the questions put by
the age and to proclaim it in ways that fit actual situations.

The priest's mission is therefore not just a mission in the
church but a mission into the world in, with, and from the

church. We would misunderstand the priest's mission if we thought it was enough to strive to hold the line. We must let ourselves be challenged by the questions put by young people and those we term lapsed. For the same reason efforts on behalf of social justice and a social order in keeping with human dignity are part of the priest's mission. Roger Schutz summarizes the pattern of Christian life demanded today in the slogan "struggle and contemplation." This is a contemporary form of the old monastic rule *ora et labora*.

It has been said that a theologian needs to have the Bible in one hand and the day's newspaper in the other, and certainly it would be a bad pastor who had no awareness of people's needs, problems, anxieties, and fears and who did not in the proper sense of the term share their life. This Christian life that, properly understood, is open to the world also includes being concerned for human education and formation and human culture, involving one's own way of life too. A spiritual life is hardly possible in the long term without intellectual life and intellectual formation.

The priest—a man of the church

There is finally a third aspect of the spiritual dimension of the priestly ministry. If the church is the place and the sacrament of the Spirit, then the spiritual character of the priestly ministry entails its churchly nature. The statement that the church is the sacrament of the Spirit does indeed mean it is not the individual ego and its subjective opinions, intentions, interests, and needs, but the larger "we" of the entire community of faith of the church that is the place and the instrument of the Spirit. The one Spirit of Jesus Christ establishes the community in the one body of Jesus Christ in which every member has need of every other. Hence for Paul a fundamental sign of the genuineness of the Spirit and for the discernment of spirits is whether it serves the building up of the unity of the church of lives in dispute or even in permanent conflict with the church. What applies above all to the priestly ministry is "Do not break the bond of unity." The priestly ministry is only possible in community with the entire *presbyterium* under the leadership of the bishop.

This kind of solidarity in the one Spirit has nothing to do with uncritical or cowardly conformism. Churchmanship does not mean simply being indifferent to or putting up with what is indefensible. It is precisely when the church is defined as the sacrament of the Spirit that there is also a legitimate place for criticism. For if the church is so defined this means it is only the sacrament and not simply identical with what it stands for—the Spirit. In the church there therefore exists a constitutive tension between its visible institutional form and its spiritual dimension. It is always at one and the same time the church of saints and the church of sinners. If it were otherwise, we, its critics, would not belong to it at all. Because there is in the church such a constitutive tension between its visible aspect and its spiritual dimension it is ultimately not a dead and rigid system but a process: it is a pilgrim church, on pilgrimage toward a fulfillment that is only eschatologically possible. Because it is a church on pilgrimage, it is not only psychologically but also theologically impossible to identify oneself totally and unrestrictedly with everything in the church as it actually is. It is precisely in one's actual involvement with the church that criticism of the church is possible and indeed necessary. This criticism takes the church at its word when it comes to the claims it makes and measures it by its own standard, the Spirit of Jesus Christ. This was the way in which the great saints criticized the church as it was in their day.

But along with a healthy distrust of institutions, including ecclesiastical institutions, there must go a distrust with regard to one's own subjectivity. Objectivity can only be attained by fitting in to a larger framework of dialogue. This membership in the church is no fixed standpoint but rather a way and a process in which there are phases of growth and maturity but also problems of growth and maturity. People belong to the church as long as they honestly situate themselves within the larger totality of the church and allow it a genuine opportunity as against their own views and opinions, as long therefore as they do not turn their own convictions into absolutes but honestly listen to what the church has to say and do not autocratically break off dialogue with it. Belonging to the church is therefore of its very nature a phenomenon full of tension. It is not because there are tensions in the church that it is today in danger. Indeed, if there were no tensions the church would be dead, for all life involves tensions (J.A. Möhler).

If the church as a whole, as well as the individual's existence within it, is understood as a way and a process, then this excludes both a flight into the future into some utopian ideal of the church, as well as a flight into the past into what is taken to be the *El Dorado* of sound tradition. At every time the Spirit is at work in the church, including the church of the present with all its problems and conflicts. The church's tradition to which we should cling is thus a living process which does not end at some particular point—neither with Pius X nor with Pius XII, as some people think, nor with the New Testament, nor with the start of the Constantinian age, as others hold. Both the extreme conservatives and the extreme progressives lack an authentic understanding of the church and its tradition, something which was already understood as a living tradition by the Tübingen school of Drey, Möhler, Hirscher, and Kuhn. It is a question therefore of clinging to the actual church of the present with all its unsolved problems and unresolved conflicts. It is this actual church for which our priestly ministry exists. It is this actual church to which the future is promised.

A prospect of hope

This leads me in conclusion to a prospect of hope. This does not mean ending by arguing away the problems and crises. But hope is something other than cheap optimism. Hope holds its own against problems and burdens. I hope it has become clear in the course of what I have said that even today there is ground for hope. Alongside the indisputable signs of crisis there are many different signs of hope: the new interest that has been aroused in the question of meaning and the question of God, the intensive reflection on Jesus Christ, the various new spiritual movements. The often one-sidedly horizontal sociological and political perspectives of the last decade now seem to be becoming dissolved again. There are more and more indications that soon we shall no longer be able to lament the lack of interest in religion: the problem will then be whether the churches are in a position to provide a credible and convincing answer to the religious questions that have been aroused and whether they can make this shift of interest in religion fruitful from the point of view of the churches. It is in this task above all that the church's ministry will have to prove itself in the near future.

It would be fundamentally wrongheaded and perverse, however, to hold that all this could come about through grimly hanging on to old positions or that we could simply go back behind all the upheavals of the last ten years. Action and contemplation will need be together. The new pastoral task thus demands intellectual and spiritual alertness, the courage to become involved in new and strange questions, pastoral shrewdness and imagination, and above all making sure that questions of the content and matter of the gospel take precedence once again over questions of method, law, and organization. If with God's help all this succeeds, then it could be that the witness of the few priests there are could once again convince many that the vocation of the priest has a future and that it is worthwhile precisely because it demands the commitment and the involvement of the whole man.

The one mystery of God in Jesus Christ remains today, through the Spirit in the church, a powerful presence for men and women in the world. We should be grateful that we have been called to serve and be stewards of this mystery.

Six

THE POWER OF CHRISTIAN LOVE TO TRANSFORM THE WORLD

The Relationship between Christianity and Society

The Problem: Christianity in Modern Society

The subject of the 1980 Berlin Katholikentag (Catholic Day), "Love Transforms Life—Love Transforms the World," sounds at first unrealistic and naive. Can one use love to solve actual technical problems in the economy, in science, in culture, the arts, politics, marriage and the family, in work and professional life? Obviously not—at least not without a considerable degree of technical knowledge and professional competence. This objection leads us straight to the fundamental question: what contribution can Christianity make to the transformation of our life and our world? Can it be more than a private motivation for tasks, solutions, and norms that non-Christians, too, see as sensible and necessary? Is it not therefore essentially confined to the consolation provided by awareness of another world in the face of the ultimate questions of human existence? Or is there a specifically Christian responsibility toward the world? What is stimulating about the theme chosen for this Katholikentag is that, starting from the core of Christian faith, it touched on the core of the crisis of orientation of contemporary Catholicism in modern society. It asked for a new definition of the relationship, or perhaps it asked anew for the old definition of the relationship, between Christianity and society, faith and knowledge, Christian salvation and human well-being, the historical and the eschatological future.

Historical Perspectives

(1) In all earlier civilizations, indeed well into the nineteenth century, there existed a symbiosis of religion and society. The fundamental rules and structure of human life and of society were given religious legitimation in all religions. In the ancient world the philosophical doctrine of natural law sought to provide a rational basis for these general religious ideas. By doing so it subjected positive law to the criterion of a law that could not be manipulated, something that bound even those in power and that could in an emergency validly be appealed to against them. The fathers of the church achieved a synthesis between the idea of natural law and the Christian message of the rule of God that was at the same time the rule of justice, truth, peace, and love. From this synthesis there emerged European humanism and civilization which in many transformations lasted until modern classical studies and until well into the nineteenth century.

In the modern age there occurred the process, which took place in several stages, of the emancipation of European humanism from the ecclesiastical, Christian, and finally also religious foundations which had provided its context. Part of the responsibility for this process of progressive secularization lay with the division of Christianity in the sixteenth century. Once Christianity could no longer serve as the framework within which everything could be integrated, people were forced to provide a religiously neutral basis for living together in peace. Religion became a private affair, and as far as their structure was concerned, the state and society became nonreligious, atheistic. The world became godless, and faith, Christianity, and the church became ever more unworldly and void of reality.

Law, freedom, conscience—all of them originally Christian ideas—were taken from their originally religious and Christian setting and brought into play to criticize Christianity. They were turned on their heads and became highly dangerous. Whenever such other values as civilization, the nation, the race were turned into absolutes, they necessarily became totalitarian and led to the suppression of human freedom. Thus it was that, in Horkheimer's and Adorno's phrase, the "Dialectic of Enlightenment" was reached in which rationality is continually transformed into blind irrationalism. The most blatant example of this kind of transformation of Christian civilization into barbarism was Nazism. In a different way Marxism too contains secularized and perverted elements of the Christian hope in salvation. Finally our entire scientific and technological civilization has roots in the Bible's faith in creation. But when the command to cultivate the earth that is rooted in the doctrine of creation is loosed from its religious justification and qualifications, we reach that cynical exploitation of nature that finally leads to the exploitation of man by man and the destruction of the conditions needed for a human existence.

In this way the alienation of religion and Christianity from society led ultimately to the dissolution of European humanism. Hegel spoke of the alienation of the state and of the system of morality it represented from bourgeois society, the "system of needs." Humans were now understood as beings lacking all mystery and made up of needs to be satisfied: the greatest happiness of the greatest number became the axiom of a pragmatic system of ethics and politics. When all-embracing frameworks of meaning disappear and the cohesive force of fundamental consensus continues to diminish, the interests of the group become overpowerful and conflicts between groups become unavoidable, with the isolation of the individual. The result is the dictatorship of consumption, the loss of meaning, the experience of nihilism, which can easily turn into the cynical exercise of terror.

(2) In the face of this threatened dissolution of humanism influenced by Christianity, it was understandable that for a long time the church failed to recognize the Christian roots and legitimate concerns of the process of emancipation and that its immediate reaction was one of defensive apologetics and attempts at restoration. In the pontifical Justice and Peace Com-

mission's working paper on "The Church and Human Rights" of 1974 it is candidly admitted that only too often the church's reaction to the modern movement for human rights was marked by hesitations, objections, and reservations. There is indeed mention of open hostility and condemnation on the part of the popes. Unfortunately this is only too true. In the nineteenth century integralism developed, a kind of religious totalitarianism which tried to derive the answer to all questions of public and private life immediately from Christian belief and subordinated all spheres of secular civilization to the guidance and control of the church's teaching office. This led to a rigidly hierarchical Catholicism shut in on itself and, at the same time, shut away from the development of society as a whole, a Catholicism with an excessive tendency toward defending rather than verifying the faith.

As early as the nineteenth century various lay movements and organizations prepared the way for a change that was given official support by the *magisterium* from Leo XIII onward. The Second Vatican Council helped these tendencies to become established. Adopting positions held by St. Thomas Aquinas, the Council explicitly recognized the autonomy of secular disciplines and affairs, while clearly distinguishing this autonomy based in creation from a false atheistic autonomy (*Gaudium et Spes*, nos. 36, 41, 56). It thus rejected secularism along with integralism and clericalism, which failed to recognize the primary competence of the laity in secular affairs (*Lumen Gentium*, nos. 21, 36–37; *Gaudium et Spes*, no. 43). Besides this, in the declaration on religious freedom, it accepted and gave a Christian legitimation to essential concerns of the modern subjective approach and thus made the step from the objective right of truth to the subjective right of the person. This does not mean abolishing the binding nature of objective truth, by which a person's conscience should be oriented; but it is recognized that only by virtue of truth does truth make its claim upon us and that it does this through the mediation of conscience (*Dignitatis Humanae*, nos. 1, 3).

The church's social teaching after the Council has decisively continued along this road. As early as 1963 *Pacem in Terris* adopted the modern tradition of human rights; the Council made this changed attitude its own (*Gaudium et Spes,* no. 41); and in *Redemptor Hominis* (1979) this grew to a carefully developed program. A similar process of critical definition and positive continuation took place with regard to the idea of social progress in *Mater et Magistra* (1961) and *Populorum Progressio* (1967), and with regard to the comprehensive liberation of humankind in *Evangelii Nuntiandi* (1975). Even the many different expressions of socialism found a differentiated appraisal in *Octogesima Adveniens* (1971).

(3) An immediate effect of the change brought about by the Council was the crisis of orientation affecting Catholicism mentioned at the beginning of this essay. On the one hand a misunderstanding of the idea of autonomy led to a temporaroy retreat to what were seen as spiritual tasks and to the church's internal problems. The result was a loss of terrain in the field of social politics. On the other hand there was an overadaptation whether to secularized bourgeois civilization or to revolutionary liberation movements. These were now seen not as a retreat from Christianity but as its secular realization. The field was dominated by the theology of secularization, by political theology, by the theology of revolution, by the theology of liberation. These latter brought into play the message of God's approaching kingdom as a critical and liberating disruption of existing conditions. Nevertheless, as a theology that was consciously and emphatically critical of society, they were able to exert merely a negative and critical influence but not to determine positively the relationship between Christianity and society.

Obviously it would not be any solution at all to try to go back and restore a precritical naive symbiosis of Christianity and society. The modern process of emancipation has also had positive results for Christianity. It has led to an increase in actual down-to-earth humanity and above all to an increase in personal freedom and social tolerance, even if in our consumer society many people are too little skilled in the right exercise of this freedom. The secularization of many originally Christian values created the necessary conditions for releasing the European Christian idea of humanity from the historical matrix in which it arose and making it universally communicable. In this way the modern age has contributed toward giving a new universal dimension to a Christianity stamped as European by its previous history, and this not least by the worldwide dissemination of scientific and technological civilization. It can perhaps become a new kind of *praeparatio evangelii* such as at one stage was provided by the Hellenistic civilization of the Roman empire.

All this calls for a new determination of the relationship between Christianity and modern society or for the renewal of the classical definition of the relationship between Christianity and modern society, between Christian salvation and human well-being. This is a long-term theological need and in what follows I can merely prepare the way with some initial indications. If in contrast to most other recent treatments this is done not under the heading of liberation but under the heading of love, then this is in reference to scripture and the treatment to be found in the classical tradition in Augustine, Thomas Aquinas, and, in another way, in Luther. What is legitimate in these modern treatments can nevertheless be integrated without difficulties in this kind of treatment.

Theological Foundations—Jesus Christ, God's Primal Sacrament

(1) This brief historical survey has shown one thing: a one-sidedly emancipatory and autonomist humanism without God leads to the destruction of human values: "It is vain to preserve a sense of absolute meaning without God" (Max Horkheimer). On the other hand it has meanwhile been shown that the process of secularization is not some natural law. Rather, the persistence of religion is a law of nature, or better, of civilization. As early as 1969 Peter Berger was talking about the rediscovery of transcendence in modern society, and at about the same time Arnold Toynbee was talking about the future of religion. Meanwhile there were many different examples of religious phenomena, often pointing in different directions, inside and outside the churches. W. Hennis could be right in saying that religion is the

major subject for the remainder of this century. A fundamental change in orientation, a conversion, is necessary.

The basic insight of the humanism both of the ancient world and of the Bible is that man is a finite being. He can only be a human human being if he does not aim at being like God, if he recognizes the limits set to him, and does not succumb to hubris. In his finiteness he cannot himself achieve the fulfillment of his being. He is dependent on others for fulfillment; he is dependent on love. In love humans experience the greatness and the misery of being human: the greatness, because love bursts the narrow confines of ego, leads them beyond themselves, and thus bestows on them fulfillment and happiness; misery, because love is very much something threatened and vulnerable and can in a thousand ways fail, be abused, be perverted. Even when it succeeds there is an element of melancholy about its fulfillment, and within it arises longing for more profound fulfillment still. In both the success and the failure of love humans experience themselves as a mystery, as a question to which they themselves do not know any answer. Ultimately they are waiting and hoping for an absolute acceptance that ultimately only God can bestow. It is only in God that the restlessness of the human heart finds its final rest (Augustine).

(2) For Christian faith Jesus Christ is the final and definitive answer to the question that humans are to themselves. As God's final and definitive revelation of himself, as the image of God (2 Cor. 4:4; Col. 1:15), Jesus Christ is at the same time the fulfillment of our being made in the image of God (Gen. 1:26), the new Adam (Rom. 5:14; 1 Cor. 15:45), in whom God finally reveals "man to man himself" (*Gaudium et Spes,* no. 22; *Redemptor Hominis,* no. 10). In him there shines forth the mystery of man that at first is only dimly and vaguely perceived; in him, too, the riddle of pain and death becomes clear. Jesus Christ is true God and true man, unalloyed and undivided (Council of Chalcedon, A.D. 451). Hence in Jesus Christ it is made clear that the highest and deepest community with God also means the highest freedom, independence, and fulfillment of the human person. Here there is no opposition between autonomy and theonomy, between self-reliance and dependence on God, as in their different

ways secularism and integralism suggest. God's love does not absorb man: rather, it accepts him and gives him the assurance of approval, setting him free to be himself. Redemption and salvation through Jesus Christ therefore means to be in community with God and the liberation of humanity.

Both these things, community with God and Christian freedom, can be summarized in the word "love." True love binds together and unites and sets people free to be themselves: in self-giving it leads to fulfillment. On the one hand love binds people to God, and on the other it is the actual realization of Christian freedom, because it is only the person who is free of himself or herself in order to be able to give himself or herself for others who is really free. Hence love of God and of neighbor is the fulfillment of the entire law (Mark 12:29–31 and parallel passages); it is the law of Christ (Gal. 6:2); the new and great commandment (John 13:34). In Jesus Christ God has revealed himself as love (1 John 4:8, 16).

The phrase "God is love" does not of course only define the hidden God by the word "love" that is accessible to human experience: this ambiguous and much-abused word is also defined by God as he has been made manifest in Jesus Christ. It is not a question of some vague universal love but of the specific love shown on the cross and made present in the celebration of the Eucharist. It is said of this love that it changes people's lives and the world.

There are three dimension to this love of God that appeared in Jesus Christ and transforms the world. First, there is a movement downward. It comes from God, who transforms the raw material of the world and fulfills it with his presence. Hence it is neither the achievement of one's own fulfillment nor striving after it but a love given that itself becomes love that gives. Second, there is a movement upward in response to God's love. In his love that gave and sacrificed itself entirely to the Father, Jesus Christ opened himself totally to the love of the Father in order to enable it to be present in freedom. Hence in worship and sacrifice Christian love recognizes the fulfillment of human freedom. Third, there is a movement laterally. In his sacrifice of himself "for many" Jesus Christ founded a new community. The

Eucharist is the sign that makes this unity present, the bond of love (*Sacrosanctum Concilium,* no. 47). The effect of Christian love is therefore representative service to the world and the life of the communion of the church. The difference between love understood in this Christian way and romantic ideas of "love" and the way in which Christian love appears as something realistic, sober, and down-to-earth is shown by Paul's paean of praise: "Love is patient and kind; love is not jealous or boastful; it is not arrogant or rude. . . . Love bears all things, believes all things, hopes all things, endures all things" (1 Cor. 13:4–5, 7).

The liberating and transforming power of this love of Christ ought not to be understood in a purely religious, nor in a purely this-worldly, manner. It embraces the whole of humankind in all its dimensions. The Christian message relativizes and transcends the usual oppositions of internal and external, private and public, this-wordly and other-worldly. The love of Christ transforms personal life and the world; it transforms joy and sorrow; it even transforms guilt into *felix culpa;* it transforms life in the world as it redeems death and turns it into a transformation into a new life. It is precisely the fact that it takes man's greatness and misery seriously and thus does justice to man as a whole that is convincing about the Christian message.

(3) All these brief indications could do with a broader and deeper theological treatment. In this context this is neither possible nor necessary, since in what follows we shall deliberately be confining ourselves to the "secular" aspects of the Christian understanding of love.

We cannot of course directly derive from Jesus Christ actual norms in the sense of immediately applicable instructions for how we should behave today with regard to secular questions. This kind of integralism would contradict the christologically founded autonomy of man and the world. What however is revealed to us in Jesus Christ is what, on the basis of God, perfect humanity is. Jesus Christ is indeed the symbol, and more than the symbol, of God as he is of humanity. Hence we derive from Jesus Christ the archetype and model, the pattern and paradigm for humanity lived and fulfilled in a Christian way, for a freedom realized in love. To put it in theological terms, Jesus Christ is God's primal sacrament for men and women.

Classical theology developed this basic sacramental idea more thoroughly with the help of the doctrine of analogy. Since what shines forth in Jesus Christ is the *ordo caritatis* in which and with reference to which all reality is created, we can use the method of analogy (not deduction) to make statements on the basis of the archetypal pattern in Jesus Christ about fundamental human and social structures. From this derives the task of Christians and of the church with regard to the world. They may not be able to offer any actual concrete solutions for the problems of today, but they must not confine themselves to general abstract principles or to personal motivation. They must make statements of substance, since these clarify in the light of Jesus Christ the vaguely open, ambiguous, and often confused phenomena of the world. Their job is to make clear by the method of sign and witness and, as it were, by providing a model of how a humanity fulfilled through love and united in love could appear.

In this sense the church is in Christ itself a sacrament; that is the sign and instrument of man's union with God as of the unity of all humankind (*Lumen Gentium*, nos. 1, 9, 48; *Gaudium et Spes*, nos. 42, 45). It is not only and not primarily through statements and documents that it is a sign but by means of its prophetic utterance and symbolic action (*martyria*), through the celebration of its worship (*leitourgia*), and above all through witness in the life of individual Christians, Christian communities, and through its entire life and its whole pattern of behavior (*diakonia*).

This sign-character of the church must not be misunderstood in a triumphalist way. The church as it actually is is always the church of sinners and stands continually in need of purification and renewal (*Lumen Gentium*, no. 8; *Gaudium et Spes*, no. 43). Given the many negative aspects of the church's history, such as its approval of slavery and the low esteem in which it held women, it is only in a self-critical manner that the church can credibly fulfill its witness toward the world. There is, too, a second point to be noted in this context. The extreme difficulty of deducing immediately applicable norms of behavior from Christian faith means that it is extremely unlikely that there can be solutions binding on all Christians. Rather, even among Christians, different solutions, party political options, and the like are possible within the common faith that is binding on all (*Lumen Gentium*, no. 36: *Gaudium et Spes*, no. 43). Finally, the church can only be a sign if it acts prophetically and pays attention to the "signs of the times," interprets them on the basis of faith, and at the same time, as the result of the questions posed by a particular age, comes to a deepened understanding of its faith (*Gaudium et Spes*, nos. 4, 11, etc.). It is precisely in its service to society that the church is God's people on pilgrimage through history, a people bound to no particular form of human civilization and to no particular political, economic, or social system (*Gaudium et Spes*, no. 43). In other words, what is involved is not an abstrct ideological system of suprahistorical principles closed in on itself, but the historical penetration and the creative transformation of the situation of the moment by the love of Christ.

Epistemological Considerations— the World in the Perspective of Love

(1) Jesus Christ gives us first of all a new way of looking at the world, a key that enables us to classify and interpret the confusing multiplicity of phenomena and what they mean, the world's contradictions, problems, and riddles. The right to this kind of "affirmational" way of contemplating the world arises epistemologically from the inner connection of knowledge and interest (Jürgen Habermas). The interest of Christians that guides their perception can be described as love. Particularly in the Augustinian tradition this inner unity of knowledge and love was taken into consideration. Among contemporary thinkers attention should be paid to Max Scheler's work on "love and perception."

True love is not blind but perceptive. Love is turning selflessly to people and to things. It therefore breaks through prejudices and obstacles to understanding. In this sense love is critical. It enables one to see reality without dissimulation; it makes one objective; it discloses reality and sets knowledge and perception free. More than this, the person who loves sees more. Love provides sympathy and sensibility and makes one conatural with what one is perceiving. St. Thomas Aquinas said *ubi amor, ibi oculus* ("where love is, there is the eye"). Hence Christian love does not aim at being a special perspective available only to those who believe; rather, it hopes to show itself to be the true vision of the reality available to everyone. To this extent it is an invitation to commit oneself to what it has found and thus to gain deeper insights into reality. In this sense it claims rationality and communicability. Let us therefore ask in what way Christian love discovers the world.

(2) We can describe the perspective of love from two points of view:

First, the perspective of love is personal. Christian love is the unqualified acceptance of the person. It recognizes every human being in his or her unique, inalienable, and absolute dignity before God. This human dignity is not tied to any race or class, any sex, any nation or religion, any political or ideological system. Christian love defends the transcendence of the human person (*Gaudium et Spes,* no. 76). For it, freedom of belief and of conscience is the most fundamental of human rights, since it provides the foundation for opposition to every kind of discrimination (racism, sexism, etc.) and every violation of the dignity of the human person (deprivation of freedom, torture, violence, etc.), for excluding every kind of totalitarianism, and for subjecting to continual revision, from the point of view of human dignity, all programs, systems, and structures (*Redemptor Hominis,* no. 17).

Love is concerned not with man or woman in the abstract but with man or woman as he or she actually is, with every individual human being with his or her unique personal dignity. This is at variance with all thinking in terms of an ideological system that often enough leads to actual human beings being sacrificed to, and indeed destroyed for the sake of, the progresss of man and mankind. Since love is concerned with every individual man or woman it is at the same time concerned about all men and women. It mobilizes imagination, understanding, and will in the cause of peace and reconciliation. Hence it rejects the use of force as a means for making sure its plans prevail. Love does not think in terms of friend and foe, with the enemy being considered and treated merely as an abstraction. It does not regard conflict as a suitable way of going about things. This does not mean opting for an unrealistic and naive idea of harmony, but rather opting for refusing to raise the class-war and conflict to the status of principles and instead trying to rob conflicts of their poison when they are unavoidable, to humanize them, and thus to provide a starting-point for reconciliation.

Second, since love is concerned with human beings and their dignity it is also concerned with their precedence over ideas, institutions, systems, and structures. Love regards the human person as the foundation, agent, and goal of all social institutions (*Gaudium et Spes,* no. 25). From this it follows that material and spiritual goods, social institutions, and the laws of the state are there for the sake of men and women and not the other way round. Love as the interest that guides our perception thus comes into conflict both with socialist and collectivist solutions and with purely capitalist, technocratic, and functionalist solutions. Love is interested in mobilizing all available knowledge and technical opportunities for the best possible improvement of men and women and their conditions of existence, not for their conditioning in the interest of economic growth, the progress of science and technology, or the victory of a particular political movement. What is involved in this is not only the fulfillment of people's material needs but also the total development of man and mankind (*Populorum Progressio,* no. 14, passim). In this respect the poor nations are very often culturally rich, while the average civilization of the developed industrial countries, as disseminated by the mass media, is culturally, morally, and religiously underdeveloped.

The primacy of the person over things and over the obligations and regulations connected with things has a threefold positive outcome. First, the goal is not simply having more but being more (Paul VI to the International Labor Organization; *Gaudium et Spes,* no. 35; *Redemptor Hominis,* no. 16). In *To Have or to Be?* (London, 1978) Erich Fromm used this axiom to derive the basis for what has been termed an alternative way of life. In our society, based on consumption and the creation of needs, this could and ought to be used as the starting-point for developing a new asceticism and frugality. This would include sacrifice and renunciation, decorum and moderation, reflection and silence. And who other than Christians should make a start? Secondly, it is a question of respecting and encouraging man as a free agent who is responsible for himself. This means people sharing in responsibility and decision with regard to the economic, social, and political processes of significance for their lives and their future (*Mater et Magistra,* nos. 65, 91; Paul VI's speech to the ILO; *Gaudium et Spes,* no. 68). It is a question of humanity being the master and not the slave of things and processes, not the slave of some anonymous fate. Thirdly, the earth's goods and resources are for everyone. Private property is therefore not some absolute and unlimited right, but has social obligations and must be fitted into the framework of the common good (*Gaudium et Spes,* no. 69; *Populorum Progressio,* nos. 22ff.). Here Christian love needs to show itself as a dynamic force that fits the demands of justice to the changing historical situation.

Are we wrong if we have the impression that for a long time now we have no longer taken for granted these principles that are taken for granted within the official social teaching of the church? Are people totally unjustified in bringing the accusation against German Catholicism as a social entity that it is lagging behind developments in the church as a whole and throughout the world? Must not Christians in our society, in one of the world's richest countries, commit themselves still more to renouncing a policy that is predominantly directed toward such purely economic goals as an increase in gross national product and a higher standard of living and reacts with delaying tactics to demands for greater international social justice and a more equitable international economic order? (Cf. the statement issued on 21 February 1979 by the Joint Conference of the German Churches for Development Questions "Justice and Solidarity in the International Economic Order.") In any case Christian love has enough in the way of critical potential and stimulation toward the future to make it unnecessary to borrow from left-wing ideologies. Christian love has no need to fall short of them in its power to transform the world.

Ontological Considerations— the World as Change

(1) The Christian option of considering the world in the perspective of love only makes sense if reality is ordered toward love and hence can be changed by love. This is the starting-point of the ontological approach. Once again it begins from the fundamental christological statement of Christian faith: God created the world in Christ and for Christ (Col. 1:16); at the end all things are to be united in Jesus Christ (Eph. 1:10). What this expresses is that the world originates in love and is ordered towards fulfillment in love. Reality is thus described not as something static, something unalterably given and unchangeable, but as history and process, as transformation through the power of love.

This kind of historical understanding of the world starts from the idea that human nature, which includes the freedom and equality of all, is extremely flexible and can and must be expressed in a variety of different ways depending on historical and cultural factors. This historical understanding does not see the world in static terms. The world is seen neither as a sacred order, a sacral cosmos (the Greek view), nor, as the totality of what is the case, as unalterable fact (the modern view), nor again as blind fate, but as an event open to the future and as history in which humanity has been entrusted with the nature with which it has been endowed to develop the world through civilization.

The ultimate source of this historical way of thinking is the Bible. It sees the world as reality that is full of hope, that lifts its head in longing and waits expectantly for the coming kingdom of freedom, for the children of God being made manifest (Romans 8). For man, created in the image of God (Gen. 1:26), finds fulfillment only in Jesus Christ, who is *the* image of God (2 Cor. 4:4; Col. 1:15). Christianity is not thinking in terms of the status quo. It sees the world as transformation through the power of love, and hence it places its trust in the transforming power of love. It believes that love is the only thing that endures (1 Cor. 13:8) and that as a result everything that is done for love is established as an enduring part of reality. The extent to which life and the world can in fact be changed by living on the basis of love, or rather on the basis of the beatitudes of the Sermon on the Mount, can be shown by examples drawn from the history of the saints.

If love is seen as the fulfillment of the world's hope, then this also means a differentiation over against a one-sidely historical way of thinking such as has often been advocated in modern times. In this approach, through a misinterpretation and misuse of the command in Gen. 1:28 to fill the earth and subdue it, nature is delivered over to unbridled exploitation. The consequences of such hubris are to be seen everywhere today. Love does not exploit nature: rather its approach is to treat it with consideration and preserve it. It cherishes and protects. It cultivates but does not manipulate. For as God's creation nature has its own dignity. This primeval human and religious attitude of reverence is something we must learn again today. Nature is not just the raw material for our ambitious plans. The attitude of pure domination must be supplemented by one of brotherhood and sisterhood whereby nature serves not humanity alone but, through it, the glorification of God. The creation psalms of the Bible and St. Francis of Assisi's "Canticle of the Sun," with its mention of "brother sun" and "sister moon," are witnesses of this kind of Christian attitude toward creation.

Christianity's understanding of history is not cyclic like that of the Greeks. History is not an eternal recurrence of the same, not an eternal becoming and passing away. Rather in the world there is something new and original, the incursion of God's love that bursts all customary molds and transcends all customary standards. But at the same time Christianity's understanding of history is not linear like that of the modern age. It does not recognize any pure history of progress, whether this be understood in an evolutionary or revolutionary sense. A history seen purely in terms of progress would be a history purely of the victors that ignored those who suffer, the oppressed, the failures, the inferiors, the dead. Love is patiently concerned with the expectation of tormented creation and brings it supremely to fulfillment. Wherever love occurs, wherever justice is practiced and peace is established, there already the kingdom of God is breaking in on us in the middle of history in a symbolic and yet real manner.

The unique and supreme example of this sacramental understanding of reality is the Eucharist, when bread and wine, "which earth has given and human hands have made," as we pray at the offertory, are the means of making present the new creation begun in the death and resurrection of Jesus Christ. For Christians this is always the pledge that love does transform the world, and it provides the strength for this to happen.

(2) Classical theology developed this historical understanding of reality with the help of the axiom that grace presupposes and perfects nature. In this context it is not possible to go into the wide variety of problems connected with the question of nature and grace today. All that need be said is that when we use the analogy of nature and grace we are not of course thinking in terms of two contiguous areas or of two layers one on top of the other, but rather of an inner relationship of presupposition and transcendence. Grace, in other words the love of God that is communicated in Jesus Christ, presupposes a nature ordered toward and appealing to love: it thus presupposes man as a person. God's grace however understands man as a being not mature but who must first be brought to perfection; this perfection is nothing other than the encounter with, and being filled by, the love of God granted man through Jesus Christ in the Holy Spirit.

The framework of this classical definition of the relationship of nature and grace allows us to focus afresh on the problem of Christianity and society. On the analogy of the classical axiom that grace presupposes and perfects nature one can formulate such statements as "Christian love presupposes human justice and brings it to perfection" (cf. *Quadragesimo Anno,* no. 137) and "Christian love presupposes human freedom and brings it to perfection" (cf. *Dignitatis Humanae,* nos. 1, 9, passim.).

(a) Christian love presupposes human freedom and justice. Love does indeed mean the unconditional acceptance of the other as a person. Love presupposes that the other can respond to love, that he or she is a person. The dignity of the human person is thus an essential element of the Christian message: it is its prerequisite and the condition for its possibility. Hence love can only be effective and bring conviction in freedom and by means of freedom. It must renounce the use of force and respect the freedom of others even when this freedom has decided differently from it or is even opposed to it (freedom of religion, tolerance). As the prerequisite and condition for its own possibility it must work for a social order in which freedom of information and communication, freedom of opinion and of assembly are guaranteed.

Similarly love presupposes justice. Love that accepts the other as a person also gives him or her what is due. In other words it fulfills the demands of justice. Love is therefore not a substitute for justice, but is an absolute determination to achieve justice for everyone. It is the soul of justice: it is the stimulus toward meeting the demands of justice under continually changing conditions.

If freedom and justice are considered as prerequisites and implications of Christian love, then this has consequences for our more detailed understanding of these concepts that in themselves can have a variety of meanings. Freedom in love and for love is not some purely individualistic freedom but freedom in solidarity. In the perspective of love justice is more than just a business of mutual good turns: it means justice directed toward the common good in a social order marked by solidarity and fraternity. If human rights are interpreted in the light of Christian freedom realized in love, then Christianity should not just be the advocate of the classical right to individual human freedom: it must work for the recognition of social, political, and cultural human rights, such as the right to work, education, consultation, joint decision-making, equality of opportunity, and freedom of movement. All this includes also the complete equality of men and women.

(b) Love brings freedom and justice to fulfillment. Freedom and justice are concepts that are still very vague and open, not to say ambiguous. They are given different and indeed contradictory interpretations today in the eastern and western worlds, in the rich industrial nations and in the poor countries of the Third World, and to some extent even in the programs of political parties. The formula "Love is the fulfillment of freedom and justice" is the Christian interpretation and "fulfillment" of these initially open and ambiguous concepts.

First of all, love brings freedom to fulfillment. Freedom is neither easy nor obvious. On the contrary, people are afraid of freedom and run away from it in a variety of ways. Hence they must first be set free and given the courage to appreciate freedom and be continually strengthened in their appreciation of it. Actual freedom presupposes a framework in which each recognizes the other's freedom. Freedom is thus realized concretely in mutual acceptance, in love. In love freedom that has been "liberated" in this way overcomes the danger that threatens today of the loss of meaning, of nihilism, and of the cynicism that finds its roots in these. It is in love, in existing for others, that freedom first experiences the fulfillment of its meaning. It is only the person who is free from himself or herself and from his or her egoism in order to devote himself or herself totally to the other who is genuinely free.

Similar considerations apply to justice. Once again it is not something obvious, since in all ages people have tended to think and act egotistically. Hence law and justice presuppose an internal state of being just. To put it in theological terms, they presuppose justification by God, inward sanctification by the love of Christ. As a result a social system based on justice alone would be cold, merciless, inhuman: *summum ius, summa iniuria.* Only love, which goes beyond the demands of justice, makes life worth living and loving. Only love experienced and handed on to others makes for human happiness.

The fulfillment of freedom and justice by love has consequences for the social and political aims that Christians set themselves. The goal cannot be a perfectly administered society run by a computer but a society that is built up from the many different cells of human society. In these cells, which are small enough for the individual to be able to grasp, the anonymity of modern society can be overcome, freedom can be experienced as meaningful and can be exercised, and one can go beyond an attitude that would see freedom merely as a demand instead of as being with other people and acting for other people in solidarity. The most important cell of such human community consists of marriage and the family. It provides the potential not just for the biological but for the spiritual, moral, and religious regeneration of society. Here the individual can experience human security and fulfillment; here love is able to transform a person's life. But it is precisely marriage and the family that today are in danger of being crushed by the objective pressures of our industrial society. In the face of the growing tendency for people to live together on a permanent basis without bothering to get married, there is need of encouragement for marriage and especially of educational, as well as social and political, help to encourage couples to think once again in terms of having children. Here Christians have an urgent task to change life and the world.

The real consequence of saying that it is only the love of Christ that brings human freedom and justice to fulfillment lies in the insight that ultimately man does not live by bread alone, that rather he is ordered and summoned toward a fulfillment infinitely surpassing everything that can be calculated, made, and thought. This vocation to the community of love with God makes man ultimately inwardly free from the tyranny of objectives, plans, claims, and interests within the world. It protects him from letting himself be made the object of such plans and aims. It bestows inner fulfillment in the midst of the disappointment, injustices, and violence of the world. When human well-being and Christian salvation are admittedly not separated but rather distinguished and differentiated from each other in this way, celebration and feasting become possible. Precisely because Christ's love is the fulfillment of freedom and justice the celebration of the Eucharist is the center and apex of Christian existence. In it the eschatological fulfillment of humanity and the world is already being celebrated in anticipation.

**The Task—Creative Renewal
of the Idea of Natural Law**

From what has been said there emerges the task of reworking in a historical perspective the permanently valid concerns of the classical doctrine of natural law. The doctrine of natural law forms part of Europe's cultural heritage. It is not therefore an exclusively Catholic or indeed merely neoscholastic concern. Its foundations are to be found in Greek philosophy, with hints in the New Testament (e.g., Rom. 2:14–16), and was accepted not just by theologians of the patristic and scholastic periods but also by theologians of the Reformation. It is to be found in an altered form once again in the right of reason and freedom in the modern human rights movement, and is also in the background of the contemporary debate about fundamental values. Finally, as has been shown above all by Ernst Bloch in *Naturrecht und menschliche Würde* ("Natural Law and Human Dignity," 1961), it has also found its way into socialist thinking.

The original concern of the idea of natural law was not some abstract deduction or the setting up of some a priori hierarchy of material values. Aristotle showed that the rights of nature could only be recognized in the *polis* because it is only in politically structured forms of living together that what man is naturally capable of being comes to development. What natural law is concerned with is the critical question about what is right in positive law, "in order, with the aid of signposts and boundary markers in the service of what is human, to act as critical disquiet in the machinery of positive law and thus to contribute towards its renewal" (A. Hollerbach).

Alongside all its indisputable services, the neoscholastic doctrine of natural law has, by its constricted understanding, unfortunately had the effect of making people suspicious of this idea of law that is fundamental for the emergence and survival of European civilization. Following the tradition of the Enlightenment (especially Christian Wolff), rather than that of St. Thomas Aquinas, it reached an abstract and rationalistic understanding tied to a legalistic view of the legal powers of the *magisterium*. Often enough the possibilities of metaphysical justification and deduction of the doctrine were uncritically exaggerated. This was connected with human nature often being considered not primarily in metaphysical terms on the basis of mind, freedom, and personality and to this extent as historical reality, but in physical and biological terms. Finally this conception lacked the perspective of the history of salvation and christology, from which there emerges a personal and historical understanding of nature that does not blockade itself against the subjectivity of the modern world but is able to accept and integrate its legitimate concerns.

The topicality of a creatively renewed idea of natural law is shown above all by the transition toward a radically emancipatory understanding of human freedom. This philosophy of emancipation overlooks the natural presuppositions of human freedom without which it cannot exist at all. It is not only the world and other people that are naturally preexisting data but ourselves too through birth. Nature is therefore everything that we have not made and that we presuppose in our making. If these presuppositions are no longer recognized, then freedom destroys itself. The nature with which we are presented is not some dead material we can manipulate as we like. Admittedly nature is ordered toward man and is entrusted to his responsibility. But in this very arrangement it is formed in a manner analogous to the intellectual, otherwise we would not be able at all to perceive and know it intellectually and to shape it technically. The way nature is directed toward man thus provides the justification for man's right to use nature in his service, but it also places limits on this. It follows that man ought not cynically to manipulate nature but rather to cultivate it with reverence. Hence the history of freedom should be understood not as an emancipation from nature but as a recollecting of nature (R. Spaemann), as the history of civilization. An idea of natural law developed on these foundations does not make biological nature as such the norm of human behavior, but nature to the extent that it provides for man's freedom as a condition of human existence and at the same time sets man the task of giving it' human realization in civilization.

The consequences of this kind of conception are literally revolutionary with regard to our technological-industrial civilization, which takes as its starting point unrestrained domination over nature and thus ends by destroying the very conditions for life. This criticism of the capitalist conditions of production is of course the precise reverse of the Marxist program of emancipation, namely the realization of a human world by returning these conditions to people themselves. Even more importantly, a natural law presupposed in freedom by freedom provides the justification for the right to life that is so important in questions of human rights in the Third World—that is the right to adequate food, clothing, shelter, and so forth. Starting from this point of view Christians must involve themselves much more decidedly in the struggle to reject an economic policy that is basically egoistic and pragmatic and replace it by a new approach. Finally, the natural law also provides the justification for the right to life of the unborn, babies, and the mentally ill. To put it the other way round, if man is defined only by his freedom then this very freedom is attacked. In that case courts or tribunals must be established to decide in particular cases on the question before them, which is equivalent to the establishment of absolute tyranny. Freedom, therefore, is only legally recognized when the natural right to life is recognized.

In today's conditions love transforms the world most of all because it lets life and everything that is be, handles, tends, cares for, and cultivates it with reverence, and allows everyone the means and conditions they need for life. The creative renewal of the idea of natural law based on the spirit of Christian love is capable of giving the political life of Europe moral substance once again and of standing for justice throughout the entire world with the aid of the fundamental idea of the tradition of European civilization. Practically the whole of this work still needs to be done.

Seven

THE THEOLOGICAL PROBLEM OF EVIL

Some Embarrassing Aspects of the Problem

The questions of demonic possession and exorcism are always divisive. The sensational treatment given to them from time to time by the mass media would not be possible if people were not secretly fascinated by the phenomena connected with them. Aspects of an archaic, magical, and mythical world that have partly been transcended and partly been repressed into the unconscious suddenly reach the conscious level once again and release suppressed fears, itching curiosity, and to some extent smug and superficial criticism. But what for our contemporary rational understanding of reality is at first so unassimilably alien gives us on closer consideration food for thought. The problem of evil and how it is overcome presents itself today just as it used to do. The increasing rationalization of our attitude to reality is continually being transformed into new forms of irrationality in a remarkable dialectic. Above all its effects are not only good: it also helps evil to organize and presents it with new, undreamed-of, ghastly opportunities. Names like Auschwitz, Hiroshima, the Gulag Archipelago speak for themselves. The questions of myth are still our questions. But what is the situation with regard to the answers?

Traditional theology took over more or less without question what scripture and the church's tradition had to say about the devil, about Satan, about demons, about evil "principalities and powers."[1] It was only with the Enlightenment that these views came in for fundamental questioning.[2] An aftereffect is the attempt by contemporary theologians to demythologize the Bible.[3] This does not mean trying to eliminate from it statements about the devil, about Satan, about demons, about evil "principalities and powers." The question is rather how these statements are to be interpreted. Are real personal entities meant, or is it a question of personifications, conditioned by the circumstances of the age, of real powers of evil? Is the devil a person or merely a cipher for a particular structure of reality or for certain psychological or parapsychological phenomena that can in principle be explained rationally today? When scripture and tradition use personal language about the evil one are they binding in faith or is it simply a question of statements about evil clothed in the language of a particular age and understanding of the world?

The theological questioning of the traditional belief in the devil coincides with the questions asked by many people, including many believers. As far as they are concerned belief in the devil in its traditional form has quite simply become no longer possible and moreover, thanks to all the various admixtures of superstition and folk-lore that are possible and not least to the rather grisly kinds of abuse to which it is liable, it has become profoundly questionable and lacking in credibility. They regard it as the residue of a magical or mythical way of thinking that has today been overtaken or at least ought to be overtaken, and with the best will in the world they cannot make anything of it. The questions that arise from theology and from contemporary experience have aroused considerable embarrassment within theology, often expressed by leaving the question of the devil more or less open.[4] The problems that arise are in fact of such importance that a mere reaffirmation of the traditional doctrine hardly seems possible.

Equally impossible is a simple negation of the traditional teaching, saying goodbye to the devil. The phenomenon of evil is an inescapable datum of experience. No pseudoenlightened optimism can delude us into ignoring the abysses in reality that raise questions for faith and for the theology that interprets this faith for those who believe. For the problem of God the phenomenon of evil is indeed existentially of fundamental importance, more than all abstract epistemological questions, more even than the admittedly important questions raised by philosophy and the critique of ideology. The experience of evil can be equally valid as an argument in favor of hope in salvation by God as it can as an argument against God: indeed, it can be a reason for reviling God. For what kind of a God is it who creates a world in which evil among men and women not only takes the form of individual weaknesses that are almost lovable, but often enough takes the form of a perverse wickedness that can assume structural and institutional forms, a world in which there are demonic lusts for power, gratification, possession, demonic cruelty, and destructive rage? Any discussion of God that does not face up to such questions remains abstract and loses any claim to seriousness and any real significance.

The way betweeen simple reaffirmation and simple negation is one of a careful and painstaking reconstruction.[5] The initial problem of such a reconstruction cannot of course be the naive question of whether the devil exists or not. Obviously the devil does not exist in the way the objects of our everyday experience or even people exist. The usual images and ideas we have, such as of the devil as a monstrous shape with goat's feet and horns, belong from the start to the realm of fairy tales and folk-lore. But putting and solving the problem in terms of rejecting such essentially frivolous, if not ludicrous, ideas does not mean in any way answering the serious question about evil. The answer to the naive question of whether the devil exists or not depends ultimately on what "exists" means in this context and thus on what it means to say that the devil exists or does not exist. Thus, the first question is how we can approach the question that has been raised in a way that does justice to the facts of the case. What is the dimension in which the question of evil and its personal appellation can be suitably asked and, if possible, suitably answered?

What follows is concerned with this question of the right dimension for raising the question of evil in a way that does justice to the facts of the case. Hence the concern is rather to disclose and illuminate the problem of evil than to provide a conclusive answer. Because of this concern much detail will have to be left open. Above all the questions concerning demoniac possession and exorcism cannot be tackled thoroughly. It is a question of disclosing the approach, of establishing the framework and the horizon, of indicating the direction in which a solution can be theologically possible. This emphasis, which, understood in the broadest sense, is that of fundamental theology, should correspond most closely to the contemporary situation of Christian belief.

Philosophical Dimensions of the Question of Evil

The first approach to the problem of evil, and the one most frequently adopted today, is based on experience. People point out that evil is a reality of human experience. There is the absurd, the horrific, the monstrous, the destructive, that which is null and faceless. It is spoken of not only in the Bible and in church tradition but also in modern literature (especially Georges Bernanos and François Mauriac, but also Franz Kafka, Albert Camus, Bertolt Brecht, and others) and the modern humane sciences (depth psychology, sociology, behavioral studies, and particularly parapsychology).[6] Ernst Bloch, Leszek Kolakowski, and Paul Ricoeur can be mentioned among other contemporary philosophers.[7] That the world is in a bad way is clearly a common human experience and complaint, and not one that can be buried by the easy optimism of an enlightened belief in progress. All this is something no one will deny. But the question is whether talking of the devil is an obligatory, or indeed at all a useful, category for interpreting this experience. Modern science thinks it is in principle capable of fitting all the phenomena connected with the devil within the framework of its theories and explanatory hypotheses without having to invoke the devil himself. But the philosphers I have mentioned reach interpretations whereby the devil is some kind of cypher for a certain structure of being or of human freedom. The argument of human experience is thus not much help on its own. What is in dispute is rather how we should correctly interpret this experience.

In order to be able to settle this dispute we need to go beyond the dimension of mere experience and venture into the realm of philosophy. In this we shall proceed in such a way that we first disclose the fundamental dimension of freedom in order subsequently to make clear by a succession of arguments how, while remaining within the dimension of freedom, one must nevertheless transcend the dimension of morality in order to do justice to the phenomenon of evil.

Our fundamental thesis is that the dimension within which the problem of evil can significantly be tackled by philosophy is that of human freedom. In contrast to physical and psychological evil (*malum physicum*), evil in the human sense (*malum morale*) only exists where there is freedom and therefore also accountability and responsibility. This thesis is directed against all attempts to solve the problem of evil simply on the basis of the way things are—structures, predispositions, hereditary factors, conditioning by one's surroundings, and similar causes. No one will dispute that all this kind of thing exists and that it needs to be taken into account in pastoral work, in education, and in jurisprudence. But if one tries to call the dimension of personal responsibility fundamentally into question with reference to these factors that undisputably share in determining people's freedom, then this ultimately leads to absurd consequences in the field of relationships between people. We can only live together in a human fashion on the basis of mutually recognizing each other as responsible for what we do. The fundamental elimination of evil as an ethical category forms ultimately a magnificent device for exculpation that is opposed to what is human, since it denies responsibility and self-determination and degrades humans to the level of things.[8] Any discussion of the phenomenon of evil must therefore take the standpoint of freedom as its starting-point if it does not want to miss the mark entirely.

The question on which everything turns for our problem is now whether we can remain in this dimension of morality. Even Kant, who stressed man's autonomy in the sphere of morality to an extent no one else has done, ran against an unfathomable mystery here. It is indicative that he gave the well-known first part of his study of religion within the limits of mere reason, published in 1793, the heading, "Of the Indwelling of the Evil Principle Alongside the Good; or Concerning What Is Radically

Evil in Human Nature."[9] In contrast to the optimism of moralists from Seneca to Rousseau, Kant detects in man a propensity to evil. This propensity to evil is, as far as he is concerned, not simply a natural datum, in contrast to preference: rather it is to be understood as a determination of free will and must be considered as freely incurred. Following Kant we can, alluding to the Bible, describe it as the perversity of the human heart. Man's propensity to evil thus has nothing to do with his sensual nature: rather it consists in the perversity of moral maxims, the perversion of the moral order. Man is aware of himself being from the start affected by evil and at the same time, if the claim to morality is not to be surrendered, he must be considered responsible for evil. For Kant this is an unfathomable mystery.

This paradox has most recently been explored afresh by Paul Ricoeur with the aim of going beyond Kant in tackling this problem. His starting-point is that we can only talk of the reality of evil in the mode of confession.[10] In confession, however, man speaks of his guilt in a way that implies this is already behind him. In confession man encounters himself as guilty. He acknowledges and confesses himself to be affected by evil. This leads Ricoeur to the paradoxical concept of the unfree will (*servum arbitrium*). What is meant by this is expressed in various images in the myths: stain, fall, Satan, etc. It is always concerned with man finding evil already there, in himself and in the world. Nobody makes an absolutely fresh start. Nevertheless it is man who sets evil in motion by surrendering to it: "To sin means to give way." In this way the form of the tempter appears on the horizon of the evil deed. For Ricoeur this form remains nevertheless a structure of man's sin. It can only be identified on the frontiers of the experience of being tempted, not outside this structure of being tempted.[11] The ontological status of this form of the tempter thus remains obscure. Nevertheless we have reached the boundaries of the dimension of morality with the realization that evil is something there ready to be encountered.

The way in which sin is a preexisting datum has traditionally been expressed in theology by the term original sin, a concept open to misunderstanding.[12] To interpret what is meant by this, most theologians today no longer rely on biological categories like inheritance but on social and ontological categories. They understand original sin as the universal situation of calamity, of being in need of salvation, that defines every human being in his or her inmost being and hence also ontologically on the basis of his or her being inextricably involved with his or her fellow human beings. On the basis of this universal human solidarity every man or woman already finds himself or herself in a situation marked by sin, guilt, and evil. The discussion of this question has ranged very widely and cannot be examined in detail in this context. In principle it remains within the dimension of personal morality: it realizes merely that the personal exists only in interpersonal relationships, so that morality exists only in the unavoidable tension of personal and social existence.

The question now, however, is whether we must not go beyond the dimension of morality, enlarged as it has been by the factor of sharing in humanity, to a more comprehensive dimension. This is in fact the case. The power of evil in humankind is not only the sum of individual evil deeds: evil does not simply heap up in order to express itself quasi-institutionally in customs, principles, bad habits, arrangements, or in the evil temper of an age, a nation, a race, or a class. Rather the element of fate, tragedy, or doom forms part of human freedom and thus of evil, as has been pointed out by Romano Guardini, Paul Tillich, Hans Urs von Balthasar, and Paul Ricoeur, among others.[13] Human freedom is not situated simply within relations between human beings. It is inextricably intertwined in the whole of reality and thus delivered over to what is disunited, sinister, and terrifying in the reality of the world. The question therefore is what is the nature of this reality that can be the arena of people's freedom as well as of their lack of freedom, that can be experienced as beneficial as well as contrary, sinister, and doomladen. To put it in traditional categories, what is the relationship between moral and physical evil?

It was above all Pierre Teilhard de Chardin who explored this question of the global conditions of good and evil. He was one of the first Catholic theologians to come to grips with the evolutionary picture of the world developed in modern times: right from the start this led him to the question of the origin of evil.[14]

The general line his answer follows is well known: in an evolutionary world which only progresses fumblingly and by a process of trial and error, evil is a statistical necessity. This applies too to evil in the sphere of what is human: human consciousness awakens in the midst of an unfinished world in a state of ferment; hence it is filled with fear and tempted either autocratically to control progress or to reject it; hence even on the path from the human to the superhuman evil is the shadow of becoming, the by-product of progress. Ultimately in evil what prevails is the original diversity against a unity becoming ever more complex and centralized. What Teilhard accepts, therefore, as the origin of evil is a nothingness understood as an undefined diversity, and creation comes into process by its progressive unification.[15] As has often been remarked, this represents an extremely problematical solution. Teilhard de Chardin himself remarked that this solution smacked of Manichaeism.[16] If evil is statistically necessarily provided by the finite nature of a world conceived of as in a state of becoming, then it coincides with the dark side of life and of reality. Physical and moral evil, *malum physicum* and *malum morale,* then refer back to metaphysical evil, *malum metaphysicum,* the finite nature of the world.

With this reference to metaphysical evil,[17] that is, to the limitation imposed by the finite nature of the world, we have reached the final and most comprehensive dimension, the metaphysical question of being. The question of evil thus faces us with the question of the meaning of being. The question arises whether infinite being is good in itself, whether the classical axiom *ens et bonum convertuntur* (being and good are identical) holds true.[18] Or is infinite being divided in itself? Does it have a propensity toward evil? This is an unheard-of intensification of the original question. We started by asking the extent to which evil "exists." Now we much conclude that the question about the existence of evil cannot be answered at all by reference to this or that individual existent but only within the context of the question about the existence of finite reality as a whole. This conclusion is not in fact very surprising, because the dimension of the question of being is also the dimension of freedom. Only in his freedom is man ordered toward the reality of being as a whole; that is, he is free with regard to individual existents. Only within the most comprehensive context possible to human thought, that of the question of being, can the question of evil rightly be put and given a suitable answer.

This comprehensive way of putting the problem of evil also involves the theological dimension of the question. The question about the meaning of being is from a theological point of view the question about the meaning of creation. Hence, looking at this from a theological perspective, we need to transcend the dimension of human freedom and move to a more comprehensive dimension, that of the freedom of God.

The Theological Perspective of the Question of Evil

The theological answer to the question of evil put in this sharper and more comprehensive form is not provided by philosophical speculation. Rather, the answer awaits the theologian in the gospel. The central message of the gospel is that in Jesus Christ God has once and for all shown himself to be the Lord of all reality, Lord over life and death, Lord too over the principalities and powers of evil, so that in faith we have the certainty that at the end God will be all in all.[19] There are no supplementary truths of the faith alongside this message of God who through Jesus Christ in the Spirit will at the end be all in all. Everything else that theologically can still and must be said is fundamentally only the development of this one central statement. In it something decisive has already been said about the reality of evil. Alongside all the revolutionary flair it may be able to obtain, evil is what is eternally outdated and obsolete, without hope. Faced with this reality the fundamental Christian attitude is not fear of evil but hope in its being ultimately and definitively overcome.

The more detailed theological development of the doctrine of evil took place within the doctrine of creation.[20] The assertion of creation is included in the central confession of God's eschatological and universal action of salvation in Jesus Christ. God can only be all in all at the end because from the beginning he is the reality that determines everything alongside which there can be no counterprinciple, nor indeed any chaos independent of God. Hence belief in creation asserts that everything that is only exists because God freely from love gives it a share in his own being. This provides a second fundamental statement about the reality of evil: in the real sense of the word evil has no independent reality. As something freely willed by God, called into being by him and maintained in being by him, all reality is fundamentally good. However violently evil may swagger and put on airs, it is theologically nevertheless empty and vain: it puffs itself up and makes much of itself but turns out to be void, hollow, and null.

The Christian doctrine of evil develops in more detail from this fundamental principle of the Christian doctrine of creation by a double process of demarcation: by the rejection of dualism and the rejection of monism.[21] Dualism (gnosticism, Priscillianism, Manichaeism) explains evil by accepting alongside God an evil principle independent of God. As is immediately obvious, this doctrine is absolutely incompatible with the Christian message of salvation. The Christian idea of God being all in all does not in any way allow for some power independent of God or opposed to him. Everything that is not God can only have its origin in him and depend on him and must therefore be seen as God's creation, which can only be created good by God. Hence it is theologically quite intolerable and indeed blasphemous to identify the finiteness and limitation belonging to creation as a finite entity with evil. Leibniz's idea of metaphysical evil is therefore more than questionable from a theological point of view.

Admittedly, the specifically Christian answer to the problem of evil only becomes clear when it is differentiated not just as against dualism but also as against monism. Monism does not recognize any independence on the part of creation with regard to the creator: it is therefore forced to trace evil back somehow or other to God himself and thus to turn God into a demon. Once again this is a striking contradiction of the holiness of God to which the Christian message of salvation bears witness. Both the dualist and the monist solutions to the problem of evil thus stand in irreconcilable contradiction to the fundamental data of the Christian concept of God and creation and represent a fundamental departure.

This double demarcation leaves very little room for a theological answer to the question of evil. There are indeed not very many models available. After dualism and monism have been excluded there is fundamentally only one possibility left: a historical definition of the nature of evil. The starting point for this classical answer is that reality has been created good by God but that evil has become reality through historical decision by creatures endowed with freedom.[22]

This historical definition of evil can only be understood against the background of the entire Christian conception of the meaning of the reality of creation. Creation is only meaningful if the freedom and goodness of God at work in it really matter in creation as what they are; in other words, if they are seen and acknowledged as freedom and goodness. The meaning of creation is thus first realized in and by means of the freedom of creation. It is only in free creatures that creation comes to itself. It is only if in creation the praise and glorification of God is sounded by free beings that creation is not some kind of meaningless self-indulgent demonstration of God's power or some kind of narcissistic reflection of the glory of the creator. To acknowledge and glorify God does not therefore limit and oppress the freedom of creation but is rather its condition. It is only in the historical decision of the freedom of creation that the meaning of the world is realized. This personal view of reality thus enables us to reach a position beyond dualism and monism, in other words a historical view of reality, or, better, one based on dialogue: in biblical terms, an understanding of reality in the perspective of the covenant. The world is not something simple but something that occurs and is constituted historically in dialogue between God and his free creatures.

For the problem of evil this understanding of reality as history on the move means that, while the reality of evil was admittedly not established by God in creation, the possibility of evil was indirectly so established. If it is God's will for the world to be freely responsible before him, then he can only achieve this by leaving it fundamentally open for his creatures to decide against him. Even God can only will freedom to the extent that he also accepts the risk involved in freedom. Indeed, the freedom of creation is clearly of such infinite value to him that the negative consequences thereby possible are of subsidiary importance by comparison. The possibility of evil does not arise from the imperfection and weakness of creation but quite the reverse, from its greatness and dignity, from what is most perfect in it: the reality of finite freedom, the reality of the person. This means however that the question posed initially of whether it is a case of evil or the evil one (or evil ones) cannot remain open theologically. To talk in purely impersonal terms of evil, of evil without a finite personal agent, is theologically untenable, because if it is followed through consistently it means either making God himself the originator of evil and thus turning God into a demon, or asserting the existence of an evil principle alongside God and thus dethroning God as God. If one excludes these two possibilities, the only possibility that remains is to understand evil as the emanation of the freedom of a creature.

A third essential statement about evil emerges from the historical definition of reality in general and of the reality of evil in particular. In doing what is evil the creature presumes to release those possibilities that God has excluded by the reality of creation, to dissolve the order of the cosmos once again and to unleash chaos.[23] In what is evil the creature gives power to the possibility excluded by God as null and void. Evil is the power in the world of what is null, chaotic, and destructive.

If one takes these considerations seriously, then the question arises whether there are other created beings endowed with freedom alongside human freedom. Are human beings alone God's partners and confederates in the world? This is not an idle question. Are humans capable of representing and accounting for the whole of reality before God? Is the anthropological perspective sufficient in view of the fact that we can never grasp the totality of reality either extensively or intensively—the first because we cannot ever know everything that is, the second because we do not know anything of what we know completely as what it is? It is therefore impossible for humans to assume responsibility for the whole of reality. If that were so, the question of the meaning of the reality of creation would arise once again.

Obviously no answers can be deduced from such questions.

If one does not want to lapse into a theology dependent on postulates, the answer to these questions can be given not speculatively but only positively on the basis of the witness of scripture and tradition. These questions are not arbitrary: they emerge from the entire context of biblical revelation. They thus expose the theological perspective within which we can meaningfully discuss the witness of scripture and tradition about the reality of angels and demons. In this perspective the mythical language of symbol that we are obliged to use in talking of angels and demons is shown to be a potential that can open up essential dimensions of our reality and that indeed has something decisive to say to us about the meaning of finite reality in general. What are involved are statements of permanent relevance.

The Permanent Relevance of the Biblical Evidence

To the question of the origin of evil the biblical evidence gives a multidimensional answer. It speaks of man's personal sin, of a power of sin dominating humankind as a whole, and of evil "principalities and powers." Even though this multidimensional answer ultimately forms a whole, it cannot be reduced to any one of its constituent elements. One cannot reduce evil either to man's personal sin alone or to the influence of evil "principalities and powers" alone without seriously diminishing the biblical evidence. The devil or demons are therefore not the only answer to the problem of evil according to the Bible. Nevertheless they are an important part of the answer. We must therefore ask what in fact is meant by this partial answer and what its relation is to the witness of the Bible as a whole.

We have not yet said anything about the actual existence of angels on the one hand and demons or the devil on the other. All we have done is to open in two ways the perspective of understanding within which this question can meaningfully be dealt with. Philosophically, it is the dimension of human freedom, which ultimately comes within the scope of the question of the meaning of being; theologically it is the question of the meaning of creation, of God's eschatological glorification by all creation. Within this twofold perspective we must now develop

what the Bible says about angels, or on the other hand, about
the devil and demons.

In trying to do this a whole new series of problems and difficulties arises, and we can only indicate them very briefly here.[24]
There is nothing specifically biblical about belief in the devil and
demons: it is part of the picture of the world that the Bible had
in common with its surrounding world, a picture of the world
that today we generally label mythological. At that time this
picture of the world was something more or less taken for
granted. Hence the existence of the devil or of demons is presupposed rather than formally taught in the Bible and in later
tradition. Corresponding to this, scripture is not aware of any
coherent demonology but simply of very different traditions that
in part contradict each other and cannot be pieced together like
a jigsaw puzzle to make a systematic demonology without ignoring their historical development. In particular, the idea of
the fall of the angels is, as far as its literary type is concerned,
a legend that occurs for the first time in the intertestamentary
writings and has only crept into the New Testament on the
margin. Hence people ask whether these statements do not need
demythologizing in the sense that one sees them as vivid por-
trayals of theological statements. In any case the traditional theological view of the devil cannot be defended today by following
the old fundamentalist method of using a concordance to cite
a whole range of scriptural texts and statements of the *magisterium* about the devil without asking to which literary genre they
belong, what is their context in terms of the history of religion,
and what was their aim and intention.[25]

This process of demythologization, or, better, this hermeneutical interpretation of the Bible, is not something one should
make too easy for oneself.[26] This kind of interpretation cannot
only have recourse to the simple pattern of kernel and husk, of
form and content. These pairs of concepts can never be properly
divided. Hence it is not just what it says about the devil and
demons but fundamentally everything the Bible says, including
what it says about God, that is conditioned by its picture of the
world. Here too there is a variety of extrabiblical influences. An
understanding of the world, of existence, or of God that is fun-

damentally not historically conditioned is an abstraction that cannot withstand critical examination in any case. Even our contemporary picture of the world is historically conditioned and limited and cannot uncritically be turned into a criterion of earlier pictures. Hence today people are more and more giving up the rationalist interpretation of myths as earlier stages of human consciousness which have now been surpassed and which date from a period when people did not know about the real causes of things. It is becoming increasingly clearer that mythical symbols are not only the form of expressing a primitive picture of the world that has today been surpassed, but represent a mode of language that discloses dimensions of reality that cannot be grasped other than by symbol. It is precisely in a world like ours, dominated by technology and increasingly becoming one-dimensional, that recalling the mythical language of symbolism has a critical and liberating function. Leszek Kolakowski talks of the contemporaneity of myth.[27] Paul Ricoeur derives the thesis, "Symbol makes one think."[28] Hence it is hardly possible simply to separate what is conditioned by its age and what is permanently valid in the Bible. It is rather a question of bringing to life the potential the symbols of mythology have to open up reality for our present world.

Such an exercise with regard to mythological statements made by scripture about angels or about the devil and demons does indeed seem to be possible on the basis of the intention of scripture in saying what it says. According to scripture the angels[29] are not, as they are for later theological speculation influenced by neo-Platonism, pure spirits without any relation to the world. They do not have a merely sporadic effect on the world varying from case to case and exercised from the outside and in a supernatural manner. Rather, they are characterized as the primeval foundations, the lords, principalities, powers, and original elements of this world and represent various different realms of God's creation. Hence their first task is the glorification of God. It is no accident that many statements about angels are to be found in liturgical texts. The "Holy, holy, holy" of Isa. 6:3 is not something we can imagine banishing from the liturgy. This liturgical evidence has greater weight than all the other statements of the *magisterium*. The angels thus articulate and realize the meaning of creation. It is quite otherwise with the devil or Satan and the demons.[30] They represent the world's resistance and revolt against God and his order and, at the same time, the hostility to man of many realms of reality. They embody the dimension of evil that is present to man and that can become a temptation for him and, if he consents to it, can gain power over him and the world. It is in this sense that according to scripture the devil is the prince of this world.[31]

This biblical view is to be distinguished from the neo-Platonic hierarchical idea of stages or ranks of being. In the view of scripture neither the angels nor the demons or the devil create any rupture in man's immediate relationship to God, personal responsibility before God, and thus man's freedom. The order of creation finds the fulfillment of its meaning in the order of salvation. This consists of the history of God's dealings with man that find their culmination in Jesus Christ. The angels, as God's messengers, have a subsidiary position of service in this history of God's dealings. Through them the whole of reality is brought into the order of salvation. Similar considerations apply to the powers of evil. They express the universal and cosmic dimension of the need of salvation and of salvation itself.[32] Historically it is only man who can set the process of catastrophe in motion by responding negatively to God's offer. But man actually does evil by surrendering to an existing power of evil instead of heading God and his order.

The angels and the devil do not therefore stand in any way at the center of the gospel but unequivocally on its margin. They represent its furthest cosmic horizon and thus provide the biblical belief in salvation with its universal and cosmic perspective, a perspective that is more a vague horizon than a content developed in detail. Hence it is literally a question of marginal truths. But this does not mean they are more or less indifferent and are arbitrarily at our disposal. The center can only be defined with reference to the framework and the periphery: without this periphery the center itself is a point lacking tension and extension. Thus, in matters of faith, it is not only what is most important that is important. What is most important, God's eschatological act of salvation in Jesus Christ, can only be lastingly maintained in its universality if the universal cosmological horizon is also maintained. Thus something decisive for the center of belief is at stake in the question of the angels as of the demons, despite all the secondary or indeed tertiary character of these truths. When the Bible speaks of angels or the devil or demons, it is using symbolic language to speak of the eschatological meaning of the world and, more precisely, of the universal cosmological meaning of Jesus Christ's act of redemption.

The Nature and Un-Nature of Evil

The relative significance and relevance of what the Bible says about the "principalities and powers" that are hostile to God and man leads to the search for a more precise definition of the essence or nature of evil. After all that has been said we can only approach this question with extreme caution and circumspection. Already from a purely philosophical point of view evil is not a categorical component to our knowledge: since the question of the meaning of being arises within it, it rather belongs to the transcendental pole of our awareness. From a theological point of view, too, what is involved is not some kind of objective knowledge but the extreme horizon of the central statements of our faith, to which, in keeping with its nature, we cannot in our treatment do full justice but which ultimately we can only express in symbolic language. From the start efforts to refine our concepts in this case cannot lead to easily managed definitions but can merely aim at a conceptual description and a hermeneutical interpretation of the symbolic language of the Bible. In this symbol and reality are not opposed to each other: rather, the definition of symbol is that it reveals reality. Ultimately evil remains a mystery understanding cannot penetrate. It is not by accident that scripture speaks of the *mysterium iniquitatis*.[33]

It follows from this that personal statements in speaking about evil may be something that theology cannot renounce; but these personal definitions cannot be made the starting point for a definition of the nature of evil, since this would fundamentally mean presenting the devil or the demons once again as some kind of actual figures.[34] The personal definitions that theology cannot do without must therefore be integrated into a more comprehensive definition of the nature of evil. The starting point of our considerations can only be the core of the biblical witness: God's universal eschatological act of salvation in Jesus Christ. Through this the evil powers and forces have finally been shown to be nothing. The real definition of the nature of evil is provided by scripture when it describes the demons as idols or nothingness.[35] Corresponding to this we shall in what follows try to interpret the reality of evil as that which is nothing in the sight of God.[36]

Only partially can one approach this understanding of evil from traditional philosophy and theology. As is known, these distinguished between absolute nothing and relative nothing, the absence of something. If in this latter case it was the question of the lack of something that essentially belonged to some important matter, then the traditional concept of *malum* emerged as a *privatio boni debiti,* the lack of some good that ought to be present.[37] But this traditional concept of *malum* is hardly sufficient to give even some understanding of the phenomenon of evil as we have hitherto encountered it both philosophically and theologically. The power of evil can hardly be explained simply by a deficiency. One must then ask what is the reason behind the lack of something that essentially belongs to some important matter. Both questions lead us to recognize the affirmational character of evil. Even more important is a second critical development of the traditional definition of evil. Evil, theologically speaking, cannot be defined in purely ontological terms as a lack of good, but only with regard to a relationship to God, that is, as a lack in the sight of God or as a perversion of the relationship to God. Evil is the creature endowed with freedom that does not recognize that it is a creature and wants to be like God. Since it seeks the meaning of its being in opposition to God, it can find this only in nothing and must therefore itself become null. Null means something other than nothing: evil is null but not nothing.

The positive result is a threefold definition of nothingness:

(1) Nothingness is the free negation of God. It is not any lack of being but a well-defined nothing: a rejection of God that takes

actual shape in the rejection of his universal will to salvation in Jesus Christ and in the sin against the Holy Spirit as the actual offer of salvation in Jesus Christ. Hence nothingness is what in both senses of the word is frivolous: what has an excessive idea of its own importance, puffs itself up and makes a lot of itself, and what thereby shows itself to be vain, empty, and null.

(2) The negation of God's being God and of his plan of salvation in Jesus Christ leads to the loss of his grace. This rejection of grace leads to a graceless existence that is condemned to itself, curses itself, and yet cannot escape by flight into pure nothingness but is rather confined to and consumed by the hell of its own nothingness. The creature's rejection of God has as consequence God's rejection, his judgment and anger. The reality of evil is thus nothingness condemned by God, finite freedom within the rejection it has itself chosen of God's judgment.

(3) From the definition of evil as negation and privation determined by God there follows another definition: evil as the perversion of itself. If the creature wishes to be like God, then as a creature it exists in a state of total perversion. Its existence depends on God and is directed toward God; it realizes this in the sense of being against God and without God. Hence evil is what is in itself contradictory, perverse, schizophrenic, totally alienated, absurd, disorganized, what is destructive and chaotic. According to the New Testament what is diabolical consists of throwing yes and no, positive and negative, into confusion: making yes to be not yes and no not no comes from the devil.[38] But the world's order is based on the distinction between yes and no. By making the absurd and crazy attempt to use negation as the foundation of his own position the devil is the "father of lies" (John 8:44), the personification of confusion and distortion. He is the sinister power of chaos in the universe created by God.

This kind of perversion of yes and no can only come from a being endowed with spiritual knowledge and free will. Both together belong to the nature of the person. The person is distinguished from other existents in that its being is given to it in consciousness and freedom. Hence only the person is able to realize or pervert the meaning of its being. If the concept of person is understood in this formal sense without including greater detail, then one cannot avoid characterizing the evil powers and forces as personally structured beings; in other words, defining them as beings of intelligence and of persistence in keeping with possessing a will. But in doing so we must of course be aware that this kind of formal concept of the person, as against its more closely defined usage in the human sphere, can only be applied in a very analogical way to both angels and demons. The devil is not some personal form but a formlessness that dissolves into anonymity and facelessness, a being that perverts itself into nonbeing: he is a person in the form of an unperson.[39] He is not to be regarded as simple and unambiguous but essentially confused and divided. Hence one cannot and should not have any firm and concrete idea of the devil. Any firm idea presupposes a clear distinction—something which, however, the devil eludes. He is therefore personal in the sense of the disintegration and dissolution of the personal. He is the proliferating destruction of himself and at the same time the destruction of all cosmic order. In this way he is indeed able to unbind and unchain the possibilities excluded in the reality of creation but he cannot remain their lord and master. They become, as it were, too much for him, so that he finds himself in the situation of the sorcerer's apprentice who cannot dismiss the spirits he has summoned. He stands under the curse and the fate of what he himself has done. This means he is not only a he but also an it. He is indeed the quintessence of the destructive impersonal forces of the world, of what is negative and chaotic in the world. It is not by accident that scripture speaks of evil "principalities and powers."[40] By this it indicates that the reality of evil is both an ego-like personally structured power and an id-like power that finds expression in anonymous systems and processes as well as in impersonal structures.

The mystery of evil cannot therefore be reduced to a single concept. What is ultimately involved are not ontological speculations but soteriological statements. It is a question not of objective statements but of statements about the horizon concerning the center of Christian belief: the message of the new creation in Jesus Christ by means of which God has once again restored peace and reconciliation not only in man but in its beginnings throughout the entire cosmos. This new beginning has finally shown the evil powers and forces to be of nothing: they are given over to derision and shame. Hence in a certain sense the devil cuts a laughable figure. Finally what is involved in the demonology of the New Testament is therefore the foundation and justification of Christian freedom.[41] Because the demons, who claim to be lords of the world, have finally been shown to be empty idols by God, the Christian is not bound to anything as far as they are concerned. He or she is liberated from any servitude to cosmic idols, liberated from the observance of cosmically-founded commandments and prohibitions, liberated from all possible ideas of tabu, liberated from fear at what is horrible in the world. This critical and liberating function of the Christian doctrine of demons has unfortunately in history very often been perverted into its complete opposite. Today we have every reason to bring this critical aspect into play both internally and externally. This brings us to the question of how to deal with evil in practice.

Coping with Evil in Practice

Christian faith, and particularly the question of evil, is a matter not just of theory but to an even greater extent one of practice. Since in the past the practical ways of coping with evil often took on alarmingly inhuman and un-Christian characteristics, the question finally arises of the practical consequences that flow from a theological reconstruction of what the Bible and tradition have to say. We shall limit ourselves to three observations that do not conclude a treatment of the problem but merely help to throw a new light on it and put it in the right perspective.

(1) It is only possible to speak of evil indirectly. Since evil is what is in itself absurd, contradictory, and nonsensical, it cannot be brought into any systematic order: a systematic demonology is impossible. More, since we have defined evil as nothingness, it cannot in principle claim any interest of its own. The devil is the complete parasite. We can therefore only speak of him indirectly as a kind of negative of the message of salvation of God's eschatological victory, as the margin and horizon of our talking

of the salvation of the world. Hence, too, in the proper theological sense of the word, we cannot believe in the devil. The act
of faith, of belief, is directed to God, to Jesus Christ, and to the
Holy Spirit alone.[42] There is no faith in the devil: belief in the
devil can fundamentally only be superstition. One cannot believe
in the devil: one can only deny and oppose him. This use of
language in the baptismal liturgy,[43] a usage that goes back to
early tradition, is in fact of the very greatest significance. It means
one can only speak of the devil in the mode of decisive renunciation. The power of the negative can only be met by the negation of the negation and, in other words, by the decisive affirmation of faith. Without this negation the affirmation would
indeed not be serious. Hence the negative way of talking of the
devil is indissolubly linked with the confession of faith involved
in baptism. It is not just some theological theory but has its roots
in the conduct of worship, which is what provides the foundation
for being a Christian and being a member of the church. Hence
it cannot either be separated from the Christian's and the
church's confession of faith.

(2) The once and for all complete renunciation of the power
of evil made at baptism must lead in the life of the baptized
Christian to a persistent attitude of watchfulness and sobriety
with regard to evil.[44] The Christian must therefore be anything
but naive and unaware: he or she must know about the reality
of evil and reckon with it in a watchful and sober way. If he or
she should think one could simply ignore the powers of evil by
following a certain pragmatism, could simply act as if they did
not exist and just not bother about them, this would betray an
extremely superficial bourgeois attitude at variance not just with
the evidence of scripture but also with many ghastly events in
our own century. It is also an offence against the sobriety that
Christianity demands to jump too quickly to the uninformed
conclusion that certain psychological phenomena (such as hys-
teria or schizophrenia) or parapsychological occurrences (telep-
athy, clairvoyance, precognition, and so forth) are to be equated
with the action of demons. The sobriety demanded by Christianity requires the consideration not just of all possibilities of a
natural explanation that may be provided by the present stance

of the profane sciences, but also the fundamental awareness that supernatural effects do not exclude but include natural causes.[45] Hence for a properly informed understanding of the faith spiritual help unconditionally presupposes medical assistance. The two forms of assistance are on a different level and cannot be played against each other. To accept or even to practice the opposite would be a sign not of faith but of superstition, which is defined as including God and, in what is admittedly a totally different way, the devil in the series of natural causes and thus completely misunderstanding their natures.

If one links watchfulness and sobriety in this way, then the fundamental possibility of demoniac possession cannot be excluded a priori. But one would have to say that there are no unequivocal theological criteria for establishing whether such demoniac possession actually has taken place in a particular case. It is theologically impossible to make an adequate distinction between demonic influence and natural phenomena or chains of causality (even if in certain circumstances extraordinary ones) because even normal and natural disasters in nature and history can be traced to the influence of the godless powers of evil.[46] The external criteria, relying on extraordinary phenomena, which the 1614 *Rituale Romanum* lays down for the determination of demoniac possession[47] are therefore in urgent need of fundamental revision. More helpful than such external criteria could be such indications for a spiritual judgment as are to be found in Gal. 5:19–23, with the contrasting lists of the "works of the flesh" and the "fruit of the Spirit." The traditional rules for the discernment of spirits point in this direction. Among signs that God is at work are love, peace, joy, inner freedom, lack of tension, patience, humility, openness, and in particular commitment to the truth. Among signs of powers opposed to God, the following could count: any behavior that is vain, haughty, destructive, and frivolous; fussiness about trivialities, disputatiousness and sullenness, reliance on force and recourse to untruthfulness. These spiritual criteria do not allow one in a particular case to accept an unequivocal and binding verdict of demonic possession. They are rather an expression of the warning always and everywhere to be sober and watchful.

(3) In coping with evil in practice the most important thing is the prayer, "Deliver us from evil."[48] The aim of theological discourse about evil is to encourage people in this prayer. It expresses both unconditional trust in the power of God and taking the powers of evil seriously. In it the power of evil is actually overcome. In it man makes room for God and his lordship. In it the meaning of creation finds realization, and thereby the reality of evil is placed in the only suitable context: that of hope in the ultimate revelation of the rule and reign of God in which all diabolical confusion, all disorder, and all trickery in the world will finally have its end.

Against the background of this "normal," everyday prayer of every Christian for delivery from evil we can reappraise and understand more profoundly exorcism, the solemn and official prayer in the name of Christ and the church for delivery from the power of the devil. This kind of exorcism presupposes medical intervention. Even in a case of "normal" illness no Christian who is reasonably well-informed about his or her faith will regard going to the doctor and praying for health as mutually exclusive alternatives. Similarly prayer for someone who is suffering does not in any case release one from the obligation to provide practical help to the extent this is humanly possible.[49] Furthermore the purpose of exorcism should not be to isolate someone and mark him or her out: the whole point of the church's solemn and official prayer should rather be to express the solidarity of all members of the church with the individual person who is suffering. Finally it cannot be a case of suggesting and inducing a pattern of behavior occurring in someone else and regarded as characteristic of demoniac possession, as seems very often to be the case in the usual form that exorcism takes. When it is correctly understood and responsibly practiced, the official prayer for delivery from the power of evil rather has the meaning of the freedom for which Jesus Christ has set us free being bestowed or restored by God on or to someone. A suitable theological theory of exorcism thus leads to criticism of many forms of current practice and to the demand for their revision.

But abuse does not do away with legitimate use. In our case it may even demand it. The church's solemn and official prayer for delivery from the power of evil in fact prevents dimensions of reality that continually arise against all one-dimensional ideologies of enlightenment being pushed down into the uncontrolled world of subcultures, and thus finally being surrendered to superstition. It prevents the individual being left alone with his or her experiences and problems of suffering, in our civilization of painlessness with its blunted sensibilities. For this reason theology must not eliminate the symbols, categories, and formulas that have been handed down for interpreting evil. Rather it must reflect on these in dialogue with modern science and thus recall them to mind in their power to disclose reality and bestow hope. It must ensure that this ability of theirs to arouse hope and liberate does not fall into forgetfulness or be perverted into its opposite. It is precisely over the question of evil that service to people demands of theologians service to the faith that has been handed down.

NOTES

1. A recent presentation of the traditional teaching is A. Winkelhofer, *Traktat über den Teufel*, Frankfurt-am-Main, 1961. Recent literature is listed in the comprehensive surveys by D. Zähringer, *"Die Dämonen," in Mysterium Salutis*, vol. 2, Einsiedeln/Zürich/Cologne, 1967, pp. 996–1019, and J. Auer, *Die Welt—Gottes Schöpfung* (Kleine Katholische Dogmatik, vol. 3), Regensburg, 1975, pp. 501–22. Unfortunately many presentations of the traditional teaching are of such hair-raising naivety that they simply offer an all too justified handle to criticism. By extravagantly exaggerating the devil's function they do more to discredit the traditional doctrine than to give a positive exposition of it. Examples are N. Corté, *Unser Widersacher de Teufel*, Aschaffenburg, 1957, and E. von Petersdorff, *Dämonologie*, 2 vols., Munich, 1956–1957.

2. Cf. Emanuel Hirsch, *Geschichte der neueren evangelischen Theologie im Zusammenhang mit den allgemeinen Bewegungen des europäischen Denkens*, Gütersloh, 1951–1960, vol. 1, pp. 206–9 (J. Weier, F. von Spee, Balthasar Bekker); vol. 4, pp. 67–68 (Johann Salomo Semler), pp. 93–96 (the dispute over the devil); vol. 5, pp. 140–44 (the Pietist reaction), pp. 327, 371 (Friedrich Schleiermacher).

3. Rudolf Bultmann's essay "New Testament and Mythology," in Hans-Werner Bartsch, ed., *Kerygma and Myth: A Theological Debate*, London, 1953, pp. 1–44, especially pp. 3–5, remains of fundamental importance. The present discussion has been determined by Herbert Haag, *Abschied vom Teufel* (Theologische Meditationen 23), Einsiedeln, 1969, [4]1973, and his *Teufelsglaube* (with contributions by K. Elliger, B. Lang, and M. Limbeck), Tübingen, 1974. This was preceded by debate over the article by J. Duquoc, "Satan—symbole ou réalité?" in *Lumière et vie* 78 (1966): 99–105, and was followed by contributions to *Concilium* 11, no. 3 (1975) (German edition; English edition not available), and *Bibel und Kirche* 1975, nos. 1 and 2 (including the instructive survey of the literature by Hermann Häring, "Satan, das Böse und die Theologen," pp. 27–30, 66–68). Also clearly to be considered in connection with this discussion is Paul VI's address of 15 November 1972, published in *Herder-Korrespondenz* 27 (1973): 125–27, and the study document on Christian faith and the teaching on demons issued by the Congregation for the Doctrine of the Faith and published in *L'Osservatore Romano* of 26 June 1975. Herbert Haag's work was reviewed by F. Zenger in *Herder-Korrespondenz* 27 (1973): 128–31; by P. Kaiser in *Herder-Korrespondenz* 29 (1975): 36–38; by Leo Scheffczyk in *Münchener Theologische Zeitschrift* 26 (1975): 387–96. and in *Theologische Revue* 73 (1977): 131–36.

4. This embarrassment finds expression above all in a third position that has recently emerged and that to some extent is advocated by theologians who earlier gave explicit support to the traditional teaching but would now like to keep the

136 Faith and the Future

question of the devil more or less open. Cf. Karl Rahner, "Bessessenheit und Exorzismus," in *Stimmen der Zeit* 101 (1976): 721–22; Otto Semmelroth, "Abschied vom Teufel? Mächte und Gewalten im Glauben der Kirche," in *Theologische Akademie*, vol. 8, Frankfurt-am-Main, 1971, pp. 48–69; Otto Semmelroth, "Der Teufel—Winklichkeit unseres Glaubens?" in *Lebendiges Zeugnis* 31, no. 3 (1976): 29–41; and W. Beinert, "Müssen Christen an den Teufel glauben?" in *Stimmen der Zeit* 102 (1977): 541–54.

5. "In our context reconstruction means that one takes a theory to bits and puts it together again in a new form in order better to reach the goal it had set itself: this is the normal . . . procedure with a theory which from many points of view is in need of revision but whose potential for interpretation has not yet been exhausted" (Jürgen Habermas, *Zur Rekonstruktion des historischen Materialismus*, Frankfurt-am-Main, 1974, p. 9; E.T. *Communication and the Evolution of Society*, London, 1979).

6. A work that has come in for a great deal of discussion of recent years is Konrad Lorenz, *On Aggression*, London, 1967 (original *Das sogenannte Böse: Zur Naturgeschichte der Aggression*, Vienna, 1963). For a working-out of its theme from the point of view of the critique of society, cf. A. Plack, *Die Gesellschaft und das Böse: Eine Kritik der herrschenden Moral*, Munich, 1967; for substantial modifications, cf. I. Eibl-Eibesfeld, *Der vorprogrammierte Mensch: Das Ererbte als Faktor im menschlichen Verhalten*, Vienna/Munich/Zürich, 1973; for a treatment from the behaviorist standpoint, cf. B.F. Skinner, *Beyond Freedom and Dignity*, New York, 1971; for a comprehensive reassessment of the entire subject with the development of both Marxist and Freudian positions, cf. Erich Fromm, *The Anatomy of Human Destructiveness*, London, 1974. For questions of parapsychology, cf. H. Bender, *Parapsychologie*, Darmstadt, 1971, and J. Mischo, "Interdisziplinäre, diagnostische und psychohygienische Perspektiven bei Fällen von 'dämonischer Besessenheit,'" in *Concilium* (German ed.) 11 (1975), pp. 188–98. Cf. the survey of the entire discussion of the problem of evil in *Concilium* (English edition) 6 no. 6 (1970).

7. Cf. Ernst Bloch, *Atheismus im Christentum: Zur Religion des Exodus und des Reichs*, Frankfurt-am-Main, 1968, pp. 318–27, and his essay "Aufklärung und Teufelsglaube," in O. Schatz, ed., *Hat die Religion Zukunft?* Graz/Vienna/Cologne, 1971, pp. 120–34, and his *Experimentum mundi*, Frankfurt-am-Main, 1975, pp. 230–38; Leszek Kolakowski, *The Devil and Scripture*, London, 1973; Paul Ricoeur, *Finitude et culpabilité*, vol. 1: *L'homme faillible*, vol. 2: *La symbolique du mal*, Paris, 1960. A similar line to Ricoeur's had already been taken by B. Welte, *Über das Böse: Eine thomistische Untersuchung*, Freiburg-im-Breisgau, 1959. A survey of the philosophical debate is provided by Werner Post, "The Problem of Evil," in *Concilium* (English edition) 6 no. 6 (1970): 105–14, and by W. Oelmüller, "Zur Deutung gegenwärtiger Erfahrung des Leidens und des Bösen," in *Concilium* 11 (1975): 198–207, and his article on "Das Böse," in *Handbuch philosophischer Grundbegriffe*, vol. 1, Munich, 1973, pp. 255–68.

8. Cf. O. Marquardt, *Schwierigkeiten mit der Geschichtsphilosophie*, Frankfurt-am-Main, 1973, pp. 62–82.

9. Cf. Immanuel Kant, *Die Religion innerhalb der Grenzen des blossen Vernunft;* E.T. *Religion within the Limits of Reason Alone*, Glasgow, 1934. On this see J. Schwartländer, *Der Mensch ist Person: Kants Lehre vom Menschen*, Stuttgart/Berlin/Cologne/Mainz, 1968, pp. 219–33.

10. Paul Ricoeur, *La symbolique du mal*, pp. 13 ff.; E.T. *The Symbolism of Evil*, New York, 1965.

11. Ibid., p. 243.
12. Cf. the survey by Urs Baumann, *Erbsünde? Ihr traditionelles Verständnis in der Krise heutiger Theologie,* Freiburg-im-Breisgau/Basel/Vienna, 1970; Walter Kasper, *Jesus the Christ,* London/New York, 1976, pp. 203–5.
13. Cf. Romano Guardini, *Freiheit, Gnade, Schicksal: Drei Kapitel zur Deutung des Daseins,* Munich, 1948; Paul Tillich, *Systematic Theology,* vol. 2, London, 1957, pp. 41 ff., 69 ff.; Hans Urs von Balthasar, "Die Gottvergessenheit der Christen: Das Tragische und der christliche Glaube," in *Hochland* 57 (1964–65): 1–11; Paul Ricoeur, *La symbolique du mal,* pp. 205 ff., 289 ff.
14. Cf. Pierre Teilhard de Chardin, "Fall, Redemption and Geocentrism," in *Christianity and Evolution,* London, 1971, pp. 36–44; "Notes on some Possible Historical Representations of Original Sin," ibid. pp. 45–55; "Christology and Evolution," ibid. pp. 76–95; "Reflections on Original Sin," ibid. pp. 224–37.
15. Cf. Pierre Teilhard de Chardin, "The Struggle against the Multitude," in *Writings in Time of War,* London, 1968, pp. 93–114; "Creative Union," ibid. pp. 151–76; "Christianity and Evolution," in *Christianity and Evolution,* London, 1971, pp. 173–86, especially p. 179; "The Contingence of the Universe and Man's Zest for Survival," ibid. pp. 221–28.
16. Cf. Pierre Teilhard de Chardin, "Creative Union," p. 163.
17. This term was of course introduced into the discussion by G.W. Leibniz in his *Essais de Théodicée sur la bonté de Dieu, la liberté de l'homme et l'origine du mal,* 1710; E.T. *Theodicy: Essays on the Goodness of God, the Freedom of Man and the Origin of Evil,* London, 1951.
18. Cf. St. Thomas Aquinas, *Summa theologiae* I q. 5 a. 3; *Summa contra gentes II:43; de Veritate* q. 21 a. 2.
19. Cf. Walter Kasper, *Jesus the Christ.*
20. For the origin of belief in creation from belief in the history of salvation, cf. among other works Gerhard von Rad, "Das theologische Problem alttestamentlichen Schöpfungsglaubens," in *Gesammelte Studien zum Alten Testament,* Munich, ³1965, pp. 137–47; A. Renkens, *Urgeschichte und Heilsgeschichte,* Mainz, ⁴1967; Claus Westermann, *Genesis* (Biblischer Kommentar, Altes Testament, vol. I/1), Neukirchen Vluyn, 1974.
21. Cf. Leo Scheffczyk, *Creation and Providence,* London/New York, 1970.
22. This aspect is above all the concern of the well-known definition of the Fourth Lateran Council of 1215: *Diabolus enim et alii daemones a Deo quidem natura creati sunt boni, sed ipsi per se facti sunt mali;* "The devil and the other demons were indeed created naturally good by God, but have become evil by their own devices" (DS 800). This statement must be interpreted strictly according to its intention of refuting the dualistic heresy of the Cathari or Albigensians. What it is saying is twofold: first, that everything that exists apart from God only exists as the result of his creative act and not as the result of any other cause, and hence everything that is has been created good; secondly, that all evil and all sin can be traced back to the free denial of a creature. It is disputed whether in saying this the Council also positively defined the existence of demons and thus whether the statement quoted above should be taken as an absolute statement or merely a hypothetical one dependent on the view of the universe then current, i.e., whether all that can be said in the way of a dogmatically binding statement is that, if there are demons, then they were created good and have become evil through the abuse of their freedom. Cf. C. Meyer, "Die lehramtlichen Verlautbarungen über Engel und Teufel," *Concilium* (German edition) 11 (1975): 184–88.

23. This is above all the direction taken by Schelling's demonology. Cf. his *Philosophie der Offenbarung,* in his collected works, vol. 14, pp. 241 ff., 256 ff., 279 ff. On this see Walter Kasper, *Das Absolute in der Geschichte: Philosophie und Theologie der Geschichte in der Spätphilosophie Schellings,* Mainz, 1965, pp. 316–26.

24. In the nature of the case most of the arguments already occur in the theology of the Enlightenment. Within the framework of contemporary discussion they have been advocated in a modified form above all by Herbert Haag.

25. This is one of the weak points of the study document of the Roman Congregation for the Doctrine of the Faith on Christian faith and the teaching on demons.

26. The points of view that Karl Jaspers brought forward against the concept of myth used particularly by Rudolf Bultmann in the debate over demythologization remain worthy of consideration. Cf. Karl Jaspers and Rudolf Bultmann, *Die Frage der Entmythologisierung,* Munich, 1954. A good conspectus of the recent discussion of myth, which has long since gone beyond the framework of the original debate about demythologization, is to be found in F. Schupp, *Mythos und Religion* (Texte zur Religionswissenschaft und Theologie, vol. 1), Düsseldorf, 1976.

27. Cf. Leszek Kolakowski, *Die Gegenwärtigkeit des Mythos,* Munich, [2]1974. The critical and liberating power of memory and recollection has recently been stated by J.B. Metz in particular, drawing from a theological point of view on Marcuse, Adorno, Habermas, and Benjamin. Cf. J.B. Metz, *Faith in History and Society,* New York/London, 1980. With regard to our question cf. W. Oelmüller, "Zur Deutung gegenwärtiger Erfahrungen des Leidens und des Bösen," in *Concilium* (German edition) 11 (1975): 198–207.

28. Cf. Paul Ricoeur, "Le symbole donne à penser," title of concluding chapter of *La symbolique du mal,* p. 323.

29. Besides the relevant entries in encyclopedias, cf. especially Eric Peterson, *The Angels and the Liturgy: The Status and Significance of the Holy Angels in Worship,* London, 1964; Heinrich Schlier, "The Angels according to the New Testament," in *The Relevance of the New Testament,* London/New York, 1968, pp. 172–92.

30. Cf. Gerhard Kittel, ed., *Theological Dictionary of the New Testament,* Grand Rapids, 1964–1976, s.v. "daimon" (vol. 2, pp. 1–20), "diaballo," "diabolos" (vol. 2, pp. 71–81), "satanas" (vol. 7, pp. 151–65); Heinrich Schlier, *Principalities and Powers in the New Testament,* Freiburg-im-Breisgau/Edinburgh/London, 1961; and for a more critical approach that takes all recent writing on the subject into account, Herbert Haag, *Teufelsglaube,* pp. 141–269, 273–388. To the extent that as a nonspecialist I can form a judgment, I find I can agree with Haag's historical exposition of the Old Testament material, but in my view his hermeneutical presuppositions are in need of criticism as are the consequences for systematic theology that flow from them. As is shown above all by his concluding remarks (pp. 503–5), his solution ends up in terms of systematic theology on the one hand by turning God into a demon, on the other by creating a sublime Manichaeism which sees evil as entailed by the finite nature of the world. That is indeed casting out demons by Beelzebub. The noteworthy New Testament contribution by M. Limbeck to this volume (pp. 273–388) is to the highest degree counterproductive as far as the author's intention is concerned. He shows impressively the extent to which statements about the devil or demons are anchored in the various New Testament traditions, so that to ignore or exclude them would open up the problem of the canon in a very fundamental way. A systematic theologian would not advise any exegete to saw off in this way the branch on

which both are sitting. Attention should also be drawn to the contribution by Karl Kertelge to this volume.

30. Cf. John 12:31; 14:30; 16:11; and also 2 Cor. 4:4.

32. Cf. 2 Thes. 2:7 (Vulgate).

33. This cosmic aspect appears in very early New Testament passages such as Phil. 2:10 and is broadly developed in the deutero-Pauline writings (cf. Eph. 1:21; Col. 1:13, 16; 2:10, 15; and 1 Pet. 3:22). On the meaning of the universal and cosmological dimensions of christology, cf. Walter Kasper, *Jesus the Christ,* pp. 185–92.

34. In this context too much value should not be placed on the concept of person or personification. What is involved is the theologically indispensable element of freedom, which admittedly discloses personal structures. The application of the concept of person—obviously merely by analogy—to the devil or the demons still needs thorough clarification. The same applies to the category of personification. In what follows the attempt will be made to show that both categories are necessary for an adequate interpretation of evil. The question is further developed by Karl Lehmann in "Der Teufel—ein personales Wesen?" in Walter Kasper and Karl Lehmann, eds., *Teufel—Dämonen—Besessenheit: Zur Wirklichkeit des Bösen,* Mainz, 1978, pp. 71–98.

35. This is shown by the fact that from the statement in Ps. 96:5 and 1 Chron. 16:26 that the gods of the heathen are idols or nothingness (*elilim*) (cf. Isa. 44:9–20) the Septuagint and the Vulgate say the gods of the heathen are demons (cf. Deut. 32:17, Ps. 106:37). The fact that the demons are idols with no real existence is made plain by 1 Cor. 8:4; 10:19–22. Cf. Gerhard Kittel, ed., *Theological Dictionary of the New Testament,* s.v. "eidolon," vol. 2, pp. 375–80; Hans Conzelmann, *1 Corinthians: A Commentary on the First Epistle to the Corinthians,* Philadelphia, 1975, pp. 142–43, 173.

36. Here I pick up a definition given and developed by Karl Barth in *Church Dogmatics,* vol. 3, pt. 3, Edinburgh, 1961, pp. 289–368. Despite all the suggestions for which I am indebted to Barth, I differ fundamentally from his position. Barth defines nothingness as a third mode of being, neither God nor creation, but what really corresponds to what God does not will, the reverse side of God's choice and approval (cf. especially pp. 349 ff.). Taking this as his starting point Barth is able to dispute the idea that angels and demons spring from a common root (cf. pp. 519 ff.). As against this kind of third mode of being, something which is probably a theological impossibility, I am concerned with the created nature of evil that has been perverted through its own decision. In this I am aware that the concept of negation or negativity that I am using stands in need of yet more precise philosophical clarification.

37. Cf. Thomas Aquinas, *Summa theologiae* I q. 48 a. 1; *Summa contra gentes* III: 7 ff.; *de Malo* q. 1 a. 1. For the history of this view cf. F. Billicsich, *Das Problem des Übels in der Philosophie des Abendlandes,* 3 vols., Vienna, 1952–1959. For a critical approach to the traditional definition of evil see Ludger Oeing-Hanhoff, "Die Philosophie und das Phänomen des Bösen," in *Realität und Wirklichkeit des Bösen* (Studien und Berichte der katholischen Akademie in Bayern, 34), Würzburg, 1965, pp. 1–30.

38. For this interpretation of Matt. 5:37, cf. Eberhard Jüngel, *Geistesgegenwart: Predigten,* Munich, 1974, pp. 39–47.

39. On this cf. Joseph Ratzinger, "Abschied vom Teufel?" in his *Dogma und Verkündigung,* Munich/Freiburg, 1973, pp. 233–34. I would however call into question whether the category of the in-between that Ratzinger introduces in

this context is sufficient. This category borrowed from Martin Buber is more suited to interpreting the reality described by the concept of original sin than to a categorical definition of the devil or the demons.

40. Cf. Rom. 8:38; 1 Cor. 15:24; Eph. 1:21; 3:10; 6:12; Col. 1:16; 2:10, 15.

41. This emerges especially from the discussion of the question of meat from victims sacrificed to idols in Corinth (cf. 1 Cor. 8:1–13) as well as from the great debates about freedom from law (cf. Gal. 4:8 ff.) and from the dispute with what were probably Gnostic tendencies (cf. Col. 2:8 ff.).

42. For this tradition that goes back to Augustine, cf. J. B. Metz, s.v. "Credere Deum, Deo, in Deum," in *Lexicon für Theologie und Kirche*, vol. 3, Freiburg-im-Breisgau, ²1959, cols. 86–88.

43. Cf. Alois Stenzel, *Die Taufe: Eine genetische Eklärung der Taufliturgie*, Innsbruck, 1958, pp. 98–108; K. Thraede, s.v. "Exorzismus," in *Reallexikon für Antike und Christentum*, vol. 5, Stuttgart, 1941, pp. 98–100.

44. Cf. 1 Pet. 5:8. In this context the doctrine of the discernment of spirits is important. Cf. the articles on "Discernement des esprits" in *Dictionnaire de théologie catholique*, Paris, 1930 ff., vol. 4, cols. 1375–1415, particularly cols. 1405–7, and in *Dictionnaire de Spiritualité*, Paris, 1932 ff., vol. 3, cols. 1222–91. Also, Hans Urs von Balthasar, "Vorerwägungen zur Unterscheidung der Geister," in *Pneuma und Institution: Skizzen zur Theologie IV*, Einsiedeln, 1974, pp. 325–39.

45. This applies in an analogical matter also to God's action in the case of miracles. Cf. Walter Kasper, *Jesus the Christ*, pp. 89–95.

46. Cf. Karl Rahner, s.v. "Besessenheit IV," in *Lexicon für Theologie und Kirche*, vol. 2, Freiburg-im-Breisgau, ²1958, cols. 298–300.

47. Adolf Rodewyk, s.v. "Besessenheit III," ibid., cols. 297–98.

48. In the interpretation of this petition from the Our Father (Matt. 6:13), a petition which probably does not come from Jesus himself, as is suggested by comparison with Luke 11:4 (cf. Joachim Jeremias, *Abba: Studien zur neutestamentlichen Theologie und Zeitgeschichte*, Göttingen, 1966, pp. 169–70), scholars are not quite sure whether the expression should be understood as masculine ("from the evil one") or neuter ("from evil"). Both interpretations are clearly possible. Cf. H. Schürmann, *Das Gebet des Herrn: Aus der Verkündigung Jesu erläutert*, Freiburg-im-Breisgau, 1977, pp. 99 ff.; G. Baumbach, *Das Verständnis des Bösen in den synoptischen Evangelien*, Berlin, 1963, pp. 75–76; Gerhard Kittel, *Theological Dictionary of The New Testament*, s.v. "poneros," vol. 6, pp. 546–62.

49. On what precisely from this point of view must be regarded as the tragic Klingenberg case, cf. M. Adler et al., *Tod und Teufel in Klingenberg: Eine Dokumentation*, Aschaffenburg, 1977.